Take Root

and Bear Fruit

L. MAXWELL OWEN

ISBN 978-1-68517-884-0 (paperback)
ISBN 978-1-68517-885-7 (digital)

Christian Faith Publishing
832 Park Avenue
Meadville, PA 16335
www.christianfaithpublishing.com

The majority of scriptures quoted in this work were taken from the New American Standard version of the Bible.

Scripture taken from the NEW AMERICAN STANDARD BIBLE®, Copyright © 1960, 1962, 1963, 1968, 1971, 1973, 1975, 1977, 1995 by the Lockman Foundation. Used by Permission. (www.lockman.org)

Occasional quotations were taken from the New International Version of the Bible.

Scripture taken from the HOLY BIBLE, NEW INTERNATIONAL VERSION. Copyright © 1973, 1978, 1984 International Bible Society. Used by permission of Zondervan Bible Publishers.

Printed in the United States of America

To the glory of God,

Who, through His grace, has given us eternal life through faith in Jesus Christ, our Lord and Savior. And to my amazing and loving husband, Ken, whose encouragement and love made this book possible.

INTRODUCTION

Out of all the plants that we choose to put in the garden each year, my favorites are the peppers—jalapeños especially! With these luscious peppers, we make hot sauce, we add them to our spicy dill pickles and hot and spicy zucchini relish, and, of course, we make pickled jalapeños. Fabulous! We live in a temperate climate, just outside of Portland, Oregon, nestled between the Pacific Ocean to the west and the beautiful and majestic Mt. Hood to the east. Mt. Hood is part of the Pacific Cascades, a chain of volcanic mountains, most of which are dormant, Mt. St. Helens being the exception. Mt. Hood rises approximately 11,200 feet above sea level and is a source of beauty and recreation for many Oregonians: skiing, snowboarding, snowshoeing, hiking, camping, and fishing, to name a few. Now if you remember your elementary science lessons on the water cycle, you'll know that clouds, heavy with water picked up in the Pacific, move inland and run up against the mountain. Before the clouds can rise up over the mountain, they must first empty their load of water—right on top of Portland and the surrounding area. Hence, it rains here—a lot! Unfortunately, peppers prefer a drier and warmer environment—so growing big, beautiful jalapeños has often been a challenge. It requires planning, purpose, perseverance, and patience—planning where and when to plant; purpose in choosing the healthiest plants; perseverance in keeping the ground warm, free of weeds, and fertilized; and patience in waiting for the harvest.

We start by choosing the best location, one that gets the sun most of the day. We've tried our peppers in different locations but, this year, tried planting some in an old cast-iron bathtub in our garden. We start by loading the tub up with fresh composted soil and adding blood meal for an added boost. We choose plants from the

Garden Center that are large and healthy and keep them in the greenhouse until the soil outside warms up to at least 60°F. Once they are planted, we cover the soil with mulch or grass clippings, which holds in moisture and heat. Often, the immature plants will produce blossoms, but we pluck these off in order for all the plant's energy to focus on its root growth. Before long, the branches of the plant start growing, and every day, they get taller and stronger. Only then do we leave the blossoms and allow the peppers to form. We continue to weed, water and fertilize; and soon these healthy, well-rooted plants produce a great bounty of large, delicious jalapeños.

We also have fruit trees in our garden: apples, pears, prunes, and plums. If you look at one of our fruit trees, you'll see large branches reaching for the sky with healthy green leaves adorning them. But what is growing above the ground is only a reflection of what is growing under the ground. The roots grow deep down into the soil, giving support and strength to what is above the ground. A tree without strong roots is easily blown over by a storm or washed away in a flood or simply withers in the heat. The roots of a healthy tree go down deep where the soil is moist and draws in nourishment for the tree, enabling it to grow and bear fruit. It is the root that stores energy through the icy cold winter and gives new life to the tree when the spring comes. So the point is this: a plant that has no root bears no fruit.

How do we apply this to our Christian life? What does a fruitful life look like? I've often thought that to be fruitful meant that I was directly teaching someone about Jesus. And while that is very true, it is not the only evidence of a fruitful life. In 1 Corinthians 3:5–11, Paul writes,

> What then is Apollos? And what is Paul? Servants through whom you believed, even as the Lord gave opportunity to each one. I planted, Apollos watered, but God was causing the growth. So then neither the one who plants nor the one who waters is anything, but God who causes the growth. Now he who plants and he who waters

are one; but each will receive his own reward according to his own labor. For we are God's fellow workers; you are God's field, God's building.

According to the grace of God which was given to me, like a wise master builder I laid a foundation, and another is building on it. But each man must be careful how he builds on it. For no man can lay a foundation other than the one which is laid, which is Jesus Christ.

So our goal is not to save souls; that's God's job. Our responsibility is to shine God's light into a dark world—to share what God has done in our life and encourage others to put their faith in Him. There are many ways to do that: feeding the hungry, encouraging the depressed, lifting up the brokenhearted, sharing with those in need, praying with and for those in sickness and peril, visiting those who are shut-in, doing chores for widows... The list goes on and on. Through these acts, you demonstrate God's love and mercy to those who don't yet know Him, and perhaps their hearts will turn to Him, and a door to share the gospel may open—remembering always that our rock-solid foundation is Jesus Christ.

But unfortunately, many Christians have a fear of sharing the gospel. Some of this, I believe, is due to the culture we live in. For many nonbelievers, religion and God are forbidden topics. "All Christians are hypocrites!" "Organized religion is a joke!" "I can't believe in a God who would send people to hell!" These statements and others like them are becoming more and more common in today's world. Because of this resistance to the gospel message, many believers are reluctant to share out of fear of rejection or even open hostility. Often this can lead us to feel impotent and stifled with regards to sharing our faith. But God never said that all people will hear the message and receive it joyfully. On the contrary, Jesus Himself was despised and rejected. He reminds us that if they rejected Him—the Son of the living God—then we can expect them to reject us as well. Whether they accept or reject Him is the choice of the individual. Our mission is to share the love of Jesus Christ and the way of salvation.

But before we can be effective in bearing fruit for God, we must first take root in our relationship with and our knowledge of our God and Savior. The idea to write this book came to me when I was reading 2 Kings. In this passage, Hezekiah, the king of Judah, had received a letter from Sennacherib, king of Assyria, threatening to destroy them completely. In his letter, Sennacherib belittled the God of heaven and boasted that there was no god who could deliver them out of his hand. Hezekiah's immediate response was to lay this letter out before the Lord and pray.

> Hezekiah prayed before the LORD and said, "O LORD, the God of Israel, who are enthroned above the cherubim, You are the God, You alone, of all the kingdoms of the earth. You have made heaven and earth. Incline Your ear, O LORD, and hear; open Your eyes, O LORD, and see; and listen to the words of Sennacherib, which he has sent to reproach the living God. Truly, O LORD, the kings of Assyria have devastated the nations and their lands and have cast their gods into the fire, for they were not gods but the work of men's hands, wood and stone. So they have destroyed them. Now, O LORD our God, I pray, deliver us from his hand that all the kingdoms of the earth may know that You alone, O LORD, are God." (2 Kings 19:15–19)

I love Hezekiah's prayer. His primary concern was not the safety of His people but that God's reputation might not be reproached. Hezekiah wanted God to have all the glory and to be known by all the nations as the only true God. God responds, assuring Hezekiah that He would be with them and, though they might suffer loss, a remnant would survive and they would again be able to take root in the land.

> The surviving remnant of the house of Judah will again take root downward and bear fruit upward. For out of Jerusalem will go forth a remnant, and out of Mount Zion survivors. The zeal of the LORD will perform this. (2 Kings 19:30)

This can be understood literally as well as figuratively. Yes, they would once again plant and harvest the land, but they would also once again be rooted in God's hand, bearing fruit for Him. The goal of this book is to help us become more firmly rooted in God and to be active in bearing fruit for Him. At the end of each chapter, there is a page of questions which hopefully can help focus our understanding of the content, as well as encourage discussion with friends and family. There is also a Bible passage at the end of each chapter to write out and commit to memory. Hopefully this book can help guide us on the path to being healthy, well-rooted plants, thriving and bearing good fruit for God.

PART 1

Take Root

CHAPTER 1

Chosen

Our England is a garden, and such gardens are not made
by singing: "Oh, how beautiful!" and sitting in the shade.[1]
—Rudyard Kipling

You did not choose Me but I chose you, and appointed you
that you would go and bear fruit, and that your fruit would remain,
so that whatever you ask of the Father in My name
He may give to you.
This I command you, that you love one another.
—John 15:16–17

Spring is an exciting time—winter has finally released its grip; the grass is turning green, sprouts are peeking up through the ground, flowering trees are starting to bloom, and daffodils are bursting out everywhere. The soil is warming up, and it's time to start getting ready for the summer growing season.

I love going to the Garden Center and choosing the plants and seeds for the garden. Walking through the aisles, we see all kinds of plants, decorative flowers, berry plants, vegetable plants, fruit trees, shrubs, and more. It is hard to control my enthusiasm, and I must keep reminding myself not to buy out the store. We choose plants that produce the fruits and vegetables that we enjoy eating and sharing. In my mind's eye, I see the end result of a thriving and bountiful

---

[1] Rudyard Kipling, "The Glory of the Garden," Public Domain Poetry, Puttock International Pty. Ltd., publicdomainpoetry.com, © 2005.

garden. In reality, we are not just buying the plant; we're buying the fruit it will produce, so we look for healthy ones with good growth. We load up our cart with all kinds of greenery, including some flowers to attract the bees and other pollinators, and we head to the checkout counter. And there we see the discount rack, the less-than-perfect plants—root-bound and dying—struggling to stay upright. We see the potential for these plants, too—they only need better soil and some care and encouragement to become beautiful and fruitful. So we pack them into the cart as well. We also stock up on fertilizers, gardening tools, gloves, sprinklers, hoses—anything that might be useful in the garden.

Second Thessalonians 2:13 tells us that we, as believers in Jesus Christ, have been chosen by God for salvation. He sees in each of us the potential fruit we will bear. We do not all look the same. Some of us are damaged and broken—spiritually dead or dying. In fact, every one of us is lost without God's saving grace. True life is found only in Him. A plant will only survive a short while in a little pot. It needs to be transplanted into rich soil, with room for growth. The same is true for each of us. We need the richness and fullness of God in order to thrive. In the garden, different plants are chosen for different purposes: some produce fruit or vegetables, some provide herbs or spices, others attract pollinators, while others discourage pests. There are many other contributors to the garden: water hoses, tools, gloves, buckets, rakes, etc. It is the same in God's garden. We each have gifts that enable us to serve effectively. Our gifts help us to bear fruit. Your fruit may not be the same as someone else's. We bear fruit according to the gifts we have received. If you have the gift of teaching, then sow those seeds. If your gift is to encourage the family of God, then plant that "spice." If you are good at attracting people to come to God, then let that fragrance go out. If you have the gift of prayer, then use it to ask God to drive away the slugs and bugs that would attack the church. If each of us uses the gifts we have been given, then we will bear the fruit God has enabled us to bear. In Matthew 25:14–30, Jesus tells the parable of the talents.

> For it is just like a man about to go on a journey, who called his own slaves and entrusted his possessions to them. To one he gave five talents, to another, two, and to another, one, each according to his own ability; and he went on his journey. Immediately the one who had received the five talents went and traded with them, and gained five more talents. In the same manner the one who had received the two talents gained two more. But he who received the one talent went away, and dug a hole in the ground and hid his master's money.
>
> Now after a long time the master of those slaves came and settled accounts with them. The one who had received the five talents came up and brought five more talents, saying, "Master, you entrusted five talents to me. See, I have gained five more talents." His master said to him, "Well done, good and faithful slave. You were faithful with a few things, I will put you in charge of many things; enter into the joy of your master."
>
> Also the one who had received the two talents came up and said, "Master, you entrusted two talents to me. See, I have gained two more talents." His master said to him, "Well done, good and faithful slave. You were faithful with a few things, I will put you in charge of many things; enter into the joy of your master."
>
> And the one also who had received the one talent came up and said, "Master, I knew you to be a hard man, reaping where you did not sow and gathering where you scattered no seed. And I

was afraid, and went away and hid your talent in the ground. See, you have what is yours."

But his master answered and said to him, "You wicked, lazy slave, you knew that I reap where I did not sow and gather where I scattered no seed. Then you ought to have put my money in the bank, and on my arrival I would have received my money back with interest. Therefore take away the talent from him, and give it to the one who has the ten talents."

For to everyone who has, more shall be given, and he will have an abundance; but from the one who does not have, even what he does have shall be taken away. Throw out the worthless slave into the outer darkness; in that place there will be weeping and gnashing of teeth.

In this parable, the master is going on a journey and chooses three of his servants to come to him. He gave to each of them an amount of money, which they were to wisely handle, hopefully to provide a good return to the master when he came home from his journey. To one he gave five talents, to another two, and to the third he gave one. A talent was a large amount of gold or silver, some say possibly equal to hundreds of thousands of dollars; but in this parable, it represents the different abilities each person is given by God. In the parable, the man gave his servants charge of his own possessions. In the same way, the gifts God gives us are His possessions, given to us that we might increase His kingdom. So the master left on his journey. While he was away, the servant who received the five talents and the servant who received the two talents both doubled the amount. When the master returned, he praised them for their efforts. The third servant, however, made no attempt to increase the one talent he had been given but instead buried it in the ground. When his master returned, the servant dug it up and handed it back to him. The master was unhappy with this servant for his lack of ambition or concern and took his talent from him. It is unclear why this third servant did not handle his talent wisely but chose to bury it. Maybe he was afraid and allowed that fear to control his decisions. Perhaps he was jealous of the other servants who received more from the master. Maybe he was angry with the master for not giving him more, so he decided to do nothing. Jon Bloom, a teacher and cofounder of DesiringGod.org calls this an issue of pride. We feel that our gift from God is somehow less than someone else's gift and choose to do nothing with what He has given us, sitting on our hands and pouting. This shows a lack of love for God and a lack of faith in His purpose for us, and because of this, the kingdom of God suffers.

> And it's all fueled by pride. All that feeling bad about myself, it's all about *me*. It's a form of self-worship. Gone is love for my Master. Gone is love for anyone else. Gone is the wonder over the grace that I received *anything* from the Master at all. Gone is the realization that even one talent is a huge amount and way more than I deserve to steward and only looks small compared to multiple talents that others have.
>
> I think that's at least one reason why the master in the parable called the less talented servant "wicked and slothful" (Matthew 25:26). The master gave the servant fewer talents, and that meant fewer opportunities and less capacity for the servant to distinguish himself, and, therefore, he saw the master as a hard, unjust man. So he buried his talent and indulged his own wicked, slothful interests and pursuits.[2]

It is too easy to look at the talents and gifts that others have received from God and feel inadequate with what He has given us. But in reality, there are just as many people looking at us in the same

---

[2]   Jon Bloom, "It's Not a Talent Show," Desiring God, March 14, 2016, Desiringgod.org.

way, wishing they had the gifts we have. All of us who have been chosen by God have been given gifts from God. Each one of them is a great blessing and given so that we can accomplish what God wants us to do. To take those gifts and bury them in the sand is displeasing to God. He gives us gifts and abilities so that we can build up and enlarge His kingdom. Everything we have is a gift from God, and nothing is our own. We came into this world with nothing, and we will leave the same way. All that we possess is given so that we can bless others and bear fruit for God. We were chosen for this purpose.

In the construction of the tabernacle recorded in Exodus, it is written how God, through the Spirit, chose faithful people and gave specific gifts to them so that they would be able to complete the structure according to His design.

> Then Moses said to the sons of Israel, "See, the LORD has called by name Bezalel the son of Uri, the son of Hur, of the tribe of Judah. And He has filled him with the Spirit of God, in wisdom, in understanding and in knowledge and in all craftsmanship; to make designs for working in gold and in silver and in bronze, and in the cutting of stones for settings and in the carving of wood, so as to perform in every inventive work. He also has put in his heart to teach, both he and Oholiab, the son of Ahisamach, of the tribe of Dan. He has filled them with skill to perform every work of an engraver and of a designer and of an embroiderer, in blue and in purple and in scarlet material, and in fine linen, and of a weaver, as performers of every work and makers of designs." (Exodus 35:30–35)

God equips us with the gifts we need to bear fruit—it is written into our spiritual DNA. He chose us before we were born to have certain gifts and abilities, for the purpose of bearing fruit for Him. In addition, He often adds to our gifts. Sometimes, He puts a ministry in front of us which He wants us to accomplish but which we feel inadequate to do. In Exodus, Bezalel was given the ability to create all the necessary, as well as beautifully elaborate pieces of the tabernacle because it needed to be done. And He didn't just give him border-line ability; He gave him extraordinary ability to create detailed and beautiful workmanship. Bezalel apparently had no previous knowledge or ability, but God provided the skill he needed to create a tabernacle adorned for the Almighty God. He will do the same for us. Each person in the family of God has a responsibility to use his or her gifts to help produce a growing and healthy body in God's kingdom.

> But to each one of us grace was given according to the measure of Christ's gift. Therefore, it says, "WHEN HE ASCENDED ON HIGH, HE LED CAPTIVE A HOST OF CAPTIVES, AND HE GAVE GIFTS TO MEN." (Now this expression, "He ascended," what does it mean except that He also had descended into the lower parts of the earth? He who descended is Himself also He who ascended far above all the heavens, so that He might fill all things.) And He gave some as apostles, and some as prophets, and some as evangelists, and some as pastors and teachers, for the equipping of the saints for the work of service, to the building up of the body of Christ; until we all attain to the unity of the faith, and of the knowledge of the Son of God, to a mature man, to the measure of the stature which belongs to the fullness of Christ. (Ephesians 4:7–13)

So each one of us in the body of Christ has been chosen by God and gifted with abilities in order to strengthen the body. When we give ourselves to this endeavor, we become united with the body of Christ. We don't all have the same gifts, but all of our gifts work together to build up the church and unite us all in faith. Together, we come to a deeper faith and a more intimate knowledge of Jesus

Christ, and we grow to our full spiritual stature. Paul encourages us in his second letter to the Thessalonians, reminding us that we are chosen by God and called to gain the glory of Christ.

> But we should always give thanks to God for you, brethren beloved by the Lord, because God has chosen you from the beginning for salvation through sanctification by the Spirit and faith in the truth. It was for this He called you through our gospel, that you may gain the glory of our Lord Jesus Christ. So then, brethren, stand firm and hold to the traditions which you were taught, whether by word of mouth or by letter from us.
>
> Now may our Lord Jesus Christ Himself and God our Father, who has loved us and given us eternal comfort and good hope by grace, comfort and strengthen your hearts in every good work and word (2 Thessalonians 2:13–17).

In God's beautiful and amazing garden, we have been chosen to fill a specific spot, and to perform a specific function. Whether you are an apple tree, a zucchini plant, a water bucket, or a humming-bird, you have been given special gifts that God can use to enlarge and enhance His garden. He has chosen you. When we make the decision to follow Him and He fills us with His Spirit, then we can bear fruit for Him. He has a plan for your life. Now it is time to prepare the soil.

Questions to Consider

Chapter 1: Chosen

1. You are chosen by God. How do these words make you feel?

_____

_____

_____

_____

_____

2. List your top five talents; what gifts has the Master left in your hands?

- _____
- _____
- _____
- _____
- _____

3. How could you use your talents to bear fruit for God?

_____

_____

_____

_____

_____

4. Has God ever given you a gift that you never thought you had, in order for you to do something for Him? Explain.

_____

_____

_____

_____

_____

Using the lines below, write out John 15:16–17. Reread it many times during the week. Try to commit it to memory.

_____
_____
_____
_____
_____
_____
_____
_____
_____
_____
_____
_____
_____
_____
_____
_____
_____
_____
_____
_____
_____
_____
_____
_____

Holy Father,

Thank You for choosing us to be members of Your family, the church. Thank You for the talents You have given us, and help us to use them for Your glory.
In Jesus's name, amen.

CHAPTER 2

The Soil

When the soil is deficient, the plants also
are deficient and weakened,
and they lose their defenses.[3]

—Charlotte Gerson

But the seed in the good soil, these are the
ones who have heard the word
in an honest and good heart and hold it fast.

—Luke 8:15

Once the plants or seeds have been chosen and are comfortably nestled in the greenhouse, then it is time to get the soil ready. After
the long winter, this can be a chore. The ground is saturated, cold,
and hard with weeds and dead roots. We start by tilling the ground,
turning it over and over—removing weeds, roots, debris left over
from the winter, and all the peanuts the squirrels planted. This step
can take some time, as the roots of many weeds can go deep into the
soil. Pesky plants, such as wild blackberries, can be hard to eradicate
as they are very persistent and can quickly take over a garden, so we
work hard to pull out all the roots. Then we blend in some compost
or other fertilizers to give the soil a boost. If the soil is too depleted,
we add some new fresh soil until we have a rich mixture of healthy
ground. When we're done with all this, the soil is healthy, soft, and
ready for planting.

---

[3] Charlotte Gerson, "Food Matters," accessed February 18, 2021, Foodmatters.tv.

The soil of our hearts is not so different. Many times, we are cold and saturated with grief or anxiety over everything that this life throws at us. Often we need some tilling of our hearts, a turning over and over that removes all that is dead or detrimental to growth. God will work on us to remove those persistent weeds that try to take over our hearts and choke out the truth. These could be weeds of false doctrine, or weeds of materialism, indulgence, pride, or self-ishness, or even people who are leading us in the wrong direction. Then He adds to the soil whatever we need in order for us to flourish. When God plants His word in us, our hearts need to be good soil. According to Luke 8:15, we need "an honest and good heart"—a heart that hears the word and believes it, that holds on to the truth of God's word. In Luke 8, Jesus tells the parable of the Sower.

> "The sower went out to sow his seed; and as he sowed, some fell beside the road, and it was trampled under foot and the birds of the air ate it up. Other seed fell on rocky soil, and as soon as it grew up, it withered away, because it had no moisture. Other seed fell among the thorns; and the thorns grew up with it and choked it out. Other seed fell into the good soil, and grew up, and produced a crop a hundred times as great." As He said these things, He would call out, "He who has ears to hear, let him hear."
>
> His disciples began questioning Him as to what this parable meant. And He said, "To you it has been granted to know the mysteries of the kingdom of God, but to the rest it is in parables, so that SEEING THEY MAY NOT SEE, AND HEARING THEY MAY NOT UNDERSTAND.
>
> "Now the parable is this: the seed is the word of God. Those beside the road are those who have heard; then the devil comes and takes away the word from their heart, so that they will not believe and be saved. Those on the rocky soil

are those who, when they hear, receive the word with joy; and these have no firm root; they believe for a while, and in time of temptation fall away. The seed which fell among the thorns, these are the ones who have heard, and as they go on their way they are choked with worries and riches and pleasures of this life, and bring no fruit to maturity. But the seed in the good soil, these are the ones who have heard the word in an honest and good heart, and hold it fast, and bear fruit with perseverance." (Luke 8:5–15)

There are four different types of soil here—four different hearts: those beside the road, those on the rocky soil, those among the thorns, and those on good soil. The seed is the Word of God. I have heard this parable my whole life and have always thought that the seed was believing in God. But the seed is the Word of God, the Bible. There are some in our world today who no longer treat the Bible as God's inerrant word. They skip over the parts that are uncomfortable and dwell on the feel-good parts. They twist it to mean what they want it to mean—to make it more palatable for a modern world. But the word of God is "living and active and sharper than any two-edged sword, and piercing as far as the division of soul and spirit, of both joints and marrow, and able to judge the thoughts and intentions of the heart" (Hebrews 4:12). A sharp two-edged sword has a dual purpose: to cut, slice, and destroy, and also to defend and protect. His word cuts between soul and spirit; it reveals what is under the surface in the same way a sword cleaves through flesh and bone, revealing the heart. But His word also defends us, protecting us from the advancing enemy. We stand strong, knowing that the One wielding this sword is God Almighty. His sword stands between us and Satan. God knows our intentions; we cannot hide our true colors from Him. His word reveals what we believe. His word will defend us, or it will cut us down. His word is powerful. This powerful word of God is the seed that is sown.

Those Beside the Road

When the word of God is taught, the seeds of the gospel fall on the ears of the people who hear. Unfortunately, however, some may not want to hear it. Because they are not seeking the truth of God's word, they don't accept it when they hear it. People beside the road don't believe because the devil snatches away the seed before they can even acknowledge it. They have already closed their ears and refuse to even listen. Jesus reminds us many times, "He who has ears to hear, let him hear." (Matthew 11:15; Mark 4:9; Luke 8:8; 14:35). Many fall into this category because they hear and believe what the world is telling them to believe and refuse to hear the truth of God's word. They dismiss His word from the start, never even allowing it to penetrate the surface of their heart. People who are beside the road are not living a life of purpose, not in the garden or on the road but beside it—living life between the two. Perhaps making no decision at all is, in effect, allowing the devil to decide for you. In any event, those beside the road do not believe and are in a lost state.

Those on the Rocky Soil

The people on the rocky soil are trying to acknowledge God but are still surrounding themselves with the world. They hear the word and believe and accept it—for a while; but temptation draws them back into the world, and they fall away. People in the church argue and debate over whether a person can lose their salvation, and I'm no authority on that. However, this verse seems to be saying that you can fall away if you deliberately choose to follow the world instead of God, or perhaps their "belief" was never genuine saving belief to begin with. I surely don't believe that God will drag us kicking and screaming into heaven if we choose to walk away. Whichever way this is interpreted, we need to be diligent. We are in the world but should not be of the world. What we choose to fill our minds with does influence how we act. Surrounding ourselves with worldly influences—crude and obscene talk; movies, music, and TV filled with murder, blood, and sexual impurity; indulgences of every kind—these things influence us, how we talk and act. We start to think it's not that bad, and we lose our sensitivity to it. Over time, our devotion to the world outweighs our devotion to Christ. Sometimes, we have to remove ourselves from situations, environments, entertainment, or even friends who would pull us away from God.

Those among the Thorns

This is a scenario all too familiar to many of us. The people among the thorns have heard the word and believe it but don't bear fruit. This starts to hit home, doesn't it? I know I have often wondered how fruitful my life is… Am I bearing fruit for God, or am I just coasting through? Are we playing the part of a Christian—praying, singing, taking Communion, sitting in church every Sunday—but not doing anything that bears fruit for God? Charles Spurgeon, an ardent preacher of the Word of God during the 1800s in London, England, wrote a book entitled *Humility and How to Get it*. In this book, he states, "Stale godliness is ungodliness. Let our religion be as warm, and constant, and natural as the flow of the blood in our veins. A living God must be served in a living way."[4] To be stale as a Christian is to admit that there are many other pleasures in this life that are far more interesting and enjoyable than having a vital and invigorating relationship with the Creator of the universe. How sad is that? What could be more critical or more important than our relationship to God? What could possibly bring more joy than knowing Christ Jesus? Everything else is temporary and fading away. He alone is eternal. It is important for us to remember that merely saying, "Lord, Lord," is not enough. Jesus says that He doesn't know these people, and if that is all there is to their faith, then they will not inherit eternal life.

> Not everyone who says to Me, "Lord, Lord," will
> enter the kingdom of heaven, but he who does

---

[4] Charles Haddon, Spurgeon, *Humility and How to Get it* (Tyndale Bible Society, 1970).

the will of My Father who is in heaven will enter. Many will say to Me on that day, "Lord, Lord, did we not prophesy in Your name, and in Your name cast out demons, and in Your name perform many miracles?" And then I will declare to them, "I never knew you; DEPART FROM ME, YOU WHO PRACTICE LAWLESSNESS." (Matthew 7:21–23)

Notice in this passage that these people were prophesying, performing miracles, and casting out demons in the name of Jesus Christ. Would it not appear to many that they were faithful followers? They were doing amazing things! They were doing these things in the name of Jesus. Miracles and prophecy and exorcisms! But just because a person seems to be doing these things in the name of Jesus, doesn't mean that they are from God. Therefore, we must be discerning. We must be careful not to quickly run after people or churches because they do great and wonderful things in the name of Jesus Christ. Look instead to how they honor God and His word. Why did Jesus tell these folks to depart from Him? They were lacking something important. They were not doing the will of God. Jesus said they were practicing lawlessness, perhaps self-serving or self-glorifying, seeking worldly recognition rather than God's. In any case, their works were not sufficient to enter the kingdom. We are not saved by works but by grace through faith in Christ Jesus. It was not their outward acts that mattered to God but their heart…their faith. A person who is led by the Spirit of God has a heart for His word, His kingdom, and His purposes. A life lived by the Spirit bears fruit for God, because that is what God's Spirit does. It is a natural response of a Spirit-led life.

What causes us to be unfruitful? According to this parable, one reason is worry. Worry chokes out a fruitful life. When we worry, we are, in essence, denying God's power to take care of everything. It destroys faith because it is the polar opposite of prayer. Paul tells us in Philippians 4:6–7: "Be anxious for nothing, but in everything by prayer and supplication with thanksgiving let your requests be made known to God. And the peace of God, which surpasses all comprehension, will guard your hearts and your minds in Christ Jesus." And Jesus Himself states in Matthew's gospel, "Do not worry then, saying, 'What will we eat?' or 'What will we drink?' or 'What will we wear for clothing?' For the Gentiles eagerly seek all these things; for your heavenly Father knows that you need all these things. But seek first His kingdom and His righteousness, and all these things will be added to you" (Matthew 6:31–33). Our world is full of stress and worry. But God tells us to stop worry in its tracks and turn to Him for everything that we need. Worry is our way of trying to control the situation, of working it over and over in our minds to try to come to a remedy or solution for the problem, and it has its roots in fear. But this is not relying on God to take care of the situation. Prayer puts our worries in the Father's hands. We no longer need to carry it. It reminds me of a song by Brandon Heath called "Hands of the Healer,"[5] in which the singer reminds us that if we are going to allow worry to rule, then why are we praying about it? On the contrary, if we are going to allow God to rule and we go to Him with our worries and lay them in His hands, then why do we continue to stress about it? So we need to run to the Father whenever we start to worry about anything and leave it in His hands. In this way, worry is no longer controlling our thoughts. "We take captive every thought to make it obedient to Christ" (2 Corinthians 10:5b NIV).

According to Jesus's explanation of the parable of the sower, a second reason that people are unfruitful is due to the riches and pleasures of life. This is all too true for many in our beautiful country of America. Prosperity abounds. For many, bigger and better is the goal. A simple house is no longer enough—bigger, open spaces with a view, top-notch furniture and appliances, manicured lawn and garden, at a level of prosperity equal to the world's standards even if it is beyond financial reach. Our automobiles, too, are a reflection of our status in society. To many people, what you drive defines you. Subaru? BMW? Mustang? Mercedes? Pickup truck? How many of us go into debt well beyond our means to gain that status? Then

---

5   Brandon Heath, "Hands of the Healer," Written by Thad Cockrell and Brandon Heath, Produced by Dan Muckala, released August 20, 2012.

there's entertainment. How much of our time, money, and attention are focused on this? Sports, boats, cruises, jet skis, eating out, hobbies…etc. Here's the point. None of these things are wrong in and of themselves. The danger is that we become so wrapped up in these things that we forget our purpose in life. Wealth and materialism are deceitful. They trick us into thinking that everything is great so long as we're surrounded by the things that make us happy. We dwell on the things of this world and forget the things of God. This is why Jesus tells us in Mark 10:23 that it is so difficult for a rich man to enter the kingdom of heaven—not because riches are inherently evil but because we tend to put our trust and happiness in our riches instead of in God. We must be careful to always keep God at the forefront of everything and to not get caught up loving the blessings of God and forgetting from Whom they come. God has blessed us with such abundance, with such a rich and prosperous life. How can we bless others with it? If our whole life is centered on our riches and pleasures, then what good are we? Is our stuff the only legacy we leave behind?

This particular verse about the soils doesn't say whether or not the thorny ground folks are saved, but it does imply that bearing fruit is the mark of a true believer. Jesus, in Matthew 7:19–20, states, "Every tree that does not bear good fruit is cut down and thrown into the fire. So then, you will know them by their fruits." We need to be aware and keep focused on what is important. Jesus goes on to say that not everyone who says, "Lord, Lord," will be saved but those who do the will of His Father. It is the will of God that we bear fruit. Let me say it again: we are not saved by the works that we do or the fruit that we bear. We are saved by grace through faith in Jesus Christ; but a life led by the Spirit of Christ will bear fruit, because that is what Jesus did, and if we have His Spirit within us, we will only naturally follow in His steps.

Those in the Good Soil

Is not this the kind of people all Christians want to be: people who hear God's word and believe it with all their heart? We hold on to it. The verse says, "Hold it fast" (Luke 8:15). This means we are not going to allow anyone or anything to come between us and God's word, or our commitment to Him. It reminds me of healthy, strong plants that are so deeply rooted that they refuse to give up the soil. No amount of tugging, yanking, or digging will cause them to release their grip. His word is the soil, and our hearts are that stubborn root that holds fast and refuses to let go. The word of God takes precedence over everything. We are people who bear fruit. We are seeking out people in need, caring for the hungry, providing for widows and orphans, reaching out to the lost around us, trying to spread the light of God into a dark world. Sometimes, I wonder if I am bearing fruit for God—if this introverted, retired schoolteacher has anything to offer Him. But, inevitably, after I pray about it, He puts a thought in my head of things I can do to encourage the people around me. This is the working of the Holy Spirit, and it's so important to listen and follow where He leads. So how do you tell the difference between the voice of God and other "voices" in your head? The answer is simple. He will never lead us astray from God's word. This is how we can discern between His voice and other voices. If the voice leads us away from the truth of God's word, we can be absolutely sure it is not God's. He calls us to take "every thought captive," so any false thought is arrested and not allowed to continue to lead us astray. May God give us all discernment. We are people led by the Spirit, concerned with the things of God. If our heart, soul, mind, and strength are centered on Him and His purposes, then we will bear fruit. It is a natural result of a Spirit-led life.

Whether the soil of our hearts is rocky, thorny, or beside the road, that is not where we have to stay. Often in the garden, we need to transplant a plant to a new spot where the plant might thrive better. The plant may struggle for a while with the invasion of being torn from the soil, but in most cases, the plant revives quickly and thrives in the new soil. In the same way if a person is not growing in their current place, it may be necessary for the *Gardener* to move them to a better location. This is for the best benefit of the person, even though it may be a shock to their system for a while. We need to learn to allow Him to move us in the direction He wishes us to go. The good news is that even if we started out in rocky soil, among the thorns, or beside the road, that doesn't have to be our final destination.

So in order for our hearts to be good soil for God's word, we must have an open heart. Our hearts need to be soft and not hardened. Hard soil is difficult to plant in. Even if you can break through the hard surface, the ground underneath is dry and barren. It is just as difficult to plant the word of God into a hard heart—a heart that refuses to acknowledge the sovereignty of God. Sometimes, the ground must be broken and turned over and over, adding fresh soil, manure, or compost to soften the ground. God, as our Master Gardener, will also turn us over and over. Sometimes, He allows us to undergo tough times, with the outcome being that we are better prepared for His word to be planted in us. Manure and compost can be stinky stuff, but the benefit to the soil is undeniable. So it is with the "manure" in our lives; it can be a benefit to draw us closer to God. Once our hearts have been softened and God's word has been planted, then the roots will start to grow.

Questions to Consider

Chapter 2: The Soil

1. In the parable of the Sower, what does the seed represent? What does the soil represent?

   _____
   _____
   _____
   _____
   _____

2. There are four types of soil in the parable: beside the road, rocky ground, thorny ground, and good soil. Briefly describe the heart of a person in each type of soil.

   Beside the road: _____
   _____

   Rocky soil: _____
   _____

   Thorny soil: _____
   _____

   Good soil: _____
   _____

3. Put a mark next to the soil that best represents where you are currently in your relationship with God and His word. Be as honest as you can.

4. List a few of your personal stumbling blocks—things that keep you from being effective at bearing fruit for God.

_____

_____

_____

_____

_____

Using the lines below, write out Luke 8:15. Reread it many times during the week. Try to commit it to memory.

_____
_____
_____
_____
_____
_____
_____
_____
_____
_____
_____
_____
_____
_____
_____
_____
_____
_____
_____
_____
_____
_____
_____
_____

Holy Father,

Soften our hearts, and help us to be good soil, striving always to please You in everything we do. In Jesus's name, amen.

CHAPTER 3

─────────────────────

The Root

Purposes, plans, and achievements of men
may all disappear like a yon cloud
upon the mountain's summit; but, like the mountain itself,
the things which are of God shall stand fast forever and ever.[6]
—Charles Spurgeon

The yearning to know what cannot be known, to comprehend
the incomprehensible, to touch and taste the unapproachable,
arises from the image of God in the nature of man.
Deep calleth unto deep, and though polluted and landlocked
by the mighty disaster theologians call the Fall,
the soul senses its origin and longs to return to its source.[7]
—A. W. Tozer

Therefore as you have received Christ Jesus the Lord, so walk
in Him, having been firmly rooted and now being built up in
Him and established in your faith, just as you were instructed,
and overflowing with gratitude.
—Colossians 2:6–7

The planting is done, and the seeds and young plants are in the
ground. Some might think the work is done, time to sit back and

───────────────

[6] Charles Haddon Spurgeon, "Unto the End," *The Sword and the Trowel* (January 1882), 3.
[7] A. W. Tozer, *The Knowledge of the Holy* (Harper Collins, November 15, 1978), 12.

relax—but there is still more to do. We add grass clippings or mulch to the top of the soil to retain heat and moisture. This is especially helpful for plants that like the heat, like jalapeños. It also helps to control weeds. In addition, we dust the plants and surrounding soil with diatomaceous earth, which is a natural sedimentary rock crushed to a fine powder, which is abrasive to insects. This is a natural way to keep pesky bugs and spiders from chewing on the tender young plants. Depending on the type of plant and our anticipated harvest, we may also add a prop for the plant to grow on, for example, putting a cage around the pepper plant, to support all those jalapeños that will be coming. After all this is done, we keep watch on the environment, being aware of weather extremes where the plants might need extra protection, such as high winds, heavy rain, hail, or scorching heat. We check on the plants daily, watering and fertilizing when needed. Before long, the leaves begin to grow, and the plants start branching out. We know then that the roots are growing well.

When the word of God is planted in our heart and we believe in Him and receive His grace and mercy, when we have been baptized into His family and His Holy Spirit inhabits us, some might think the work is done, time to sit back and relax—but there is still work to do. Don't misunderstand me here—we are saved by grace through faith, not by works. Ephesians 2:8–9 states this clearly: "For by grace you have been saved through faith; and that not of yourselves, it is the gift of God; not as a result of works, so that no one may boast." The work we do does not save us but helps our roots to grow deeper into the soil of God's word. Keep reading in Ephesians 2:10, which states, "For we are His workmanship, created in Christ Jesus for good works, which God prepared beforehand so that we would walk in them." He is working on us so that we can do good works. God has work that He has prepared for us to do; we were created for that purpose. The works don't save us, but they are a natural outcome of a Spirit-controlled life. You will hear me say this often in this book. It is a repeated theme. If you have the Spirit of God, you will do what the Spirit leads you to do. James, in his epistle, states that faith without works is dead (James 2:17, 26). How we live our life after we are saved is evidence of our salvation. The result of a Spirit-led life is that we bear fruit. If we don't bear fruit, can we truly say we have the Spirit of God?

How does the Spirit of Christ control us? How does He cultivate the soil of our heart? It starts by having a relationship with Him. According to Jesus, the greatest commandment in the Bible is to love the Lord our God with all of our heart, soul, mind, and strength (Mark 12:30). The heart of a Christian is the heart of God. There is an old hymn entitled *Be Thou My Vision* that speaks to this amazing love.

> Be thou my vision, O Lord of my heart
> Naught be all else to me, save that Thou art;
> Thou my best thought, by day or by night
> Waking or sleeping, Thy presence my light.
>
> Be Thou my wisdom, and Thou my true word
> I ever with Thee and Thou with me, Lord;
> Thou my great Father, and I Thy true son
> Thou in me dwelling and I with Thee one.
>
> Riches I heed not, nor vain, empty praise
> Thou mine inheritance, now and always;
> Thou and Thou only first in my heart
> High King of heaven, my treasure Thou art.
>
> High King of heaven, my victory won
> May I reach heaven's joys, O bright heaven's sun;
> Heart of my own heart, whatever befall
> Still be my vision, O Ruler of all.[8]

I love the phrases "Thou and Thou only first in my heart" and "Heart of my own heart." These phrases express the deep love that the author had for God and that we should seek to have as well. Having

---

[8] Mary Byrne and Eleanor Hull, *Be Thou My Vision*, Music: "Slane" traditional Irish tune, Public Domain, © 1905, 1912.

a deep and abiding love for God is imperative for the Christian life, and it is the most amazing and beautiful part of being a Christian. Loving the Father not only involves having a heart that follows after Him but also a heart that acknowledges His sovereignty. He is God. There is no other. He has all the authority. We have no right to go against Him or His word and still call ourselves His people. He is Lord. We owe everything to Him. If we disagree with anything the Bible says, then we are wrong, because He and His word are inerrant. This is not a popular view in today's culture. Even many churches attempt to morph the Scriptures to fit the modern mindset. But this does not show love to our God or honor Him. His word is authoritative. He is Sovereign. He is our loving and good Father; and He is King, Creator, and Ruler of the universe. Charles Spurgeon had this to say about the sovereignty of God:

> Men will allow God to be everywhere but on his throne. They will allow him to be in his workshop to fashion worlds and make stars. They will allow Him to be in His almonry to dispense His alms and bestow his bounties. They will allow Him to sustain the earth and bear up the pillars thereof, or light the lamps of heaven, or rule the waves of the ever-moving ocean; but when God ascends His throne, His creatures then gnash their teeth. And we proclaim an enthroned God, and His right to do as He wills with His own, to dispose of His creatures as He thinks well, without consulting them in the matter; then it is that we are hissed and execrated, and then it is that men turn a deaf ear to us, for God on His throne is not the God they love. But it is God upon the throne that we love to preach. It is God upon His throne whom we trust.[9]

---

[9] Charles Haddon, Spurgeon, "Divine Sovereignty," *New Park Street Pulpit*, volume 2, The Spurgeon Center (May 4, 1856), spurgeon.org.

To have a good relationship with the Father, it is imperative that we love Him unconditionally and that we allow Him to be the Lord of our lives without reservation. He is our All in all. Surrendering to His authority is easier when we die to ourselves. It is our sinful nature that believes we know better than our Creator. We must daily die to ourselves and remember that it is God, Whose ways are higher than our ways and Whose thoughts are greater than our thoughts, Whom we serve. He is not our equal; He is our Master and King. Through His great love and mercy and the sacrifice of Jesus Christ, we can have a personal relationship with this awesome and mighty God!

> For this reason I bow my knees before the Father, from whom every family in heaven and on earth derives its name, that He would grant you, according to the riches of His glory, to be strengthened with power through His Spirit in the inner man, so that Christ may dwell in your hearts through faith; and that you, being rooted and grounded in love, may be able to comprehend with all the saints what is the breadth and length and height and depth, and to know the love of Christ which surpasses knowledge, that you may be filled up to all the fullness of God. (Ephesians 3:14–19)

What a great gift, one that should never be taken for granted. Relationship with Him should be the first and foremost goal of our lives. All healthy relationships depend on good daily communication. You can't expect to get close to someone with whom you never talk, so talking to God throughout every day is very important. Prayer can take many forms; it can be written, verbal or silent, long or short, public or private, petition or praise, with many words or no words at all. Through prayer, we acknowledge the *sovereignty* of God and His authority over our lives, and we give Him our worries and fears. In prayer, we ask for healing and God's intervention in our struggles. We grow in our relationship with God when we spend time with

Him in prayer. In 1 Thessalonians 5:16, we are told to pray without ceasing, to never give up on the power of prayer. We keep the lines of communication open between ourselves and the Creator of the universe.

The Bible is filled with commands and instructions on how to pray. Jesus, in Matthew 6, tells us not to make a show of prayer, like the hypocrites do; people whose only purpose for prayer is to be oohed and ahhed at by other people.

> When you pray, you are not to be like the hypocrites; for they love to stand and pray in the synagogues and on the street corners so that they may be seen by men. Truly I say to you, they have their reward in full. But you, when you pray, go into your inner room, close your door and pray to your Father who is in secret, and your Father who sees what is done in secret will reward you.
>
> And when you are praying, do not use meaningless repetition as the Gentiles do, for they suppose that they will be heard for their many words. So do not be like them; for your Father knows what you need before you ask Him. (Matthew 6:5–8)

They use beautiful and eloquent language to impress those watching, but that is the only benefit they will receive from that kind of praying. In contrast, Jesus instructs us to go into a room and close the door and pray to God in private. Beautiful, eloquent words are not needed, for God, through His Spirit within us, hears the groaning of our hearts (Romans 8:26). In fact, some of my deepest and most intimate prayer times have been when words simply would not come, and I just poured my tears out before Him. The Spirit carries these prayers to the Father, translating them into the appropriate words to convey the burden on our hearts. In Matthew 6:9–13, Jesus teaches His disciples how to pray.

> Pray, then, in this way:
> "Our Father who is in heaven,
> Hallowed be Your name.
> Your kingdom come.
> Your will be done,
> On earth as it is in heaven.
> Give us this day our daily bread.
> And forgive us our debts, as we also have forgiven
> our debtors.
> And do not lead us into temptation, but deliver
> us from evil. [For Yours is the kingdom and the
> power and the glory forever. Amen.]"

Jesus gave us this simple yet eloquent example of prayer, not that we must restate it verbatim, although there is nothing wrong with that; but I think this prayer can also be used as a template for prayer—a guide for us to follow.

"Our Father Who is in heaven, hallowed be Your name..."

It starts out by acknowledging the One to Whom you are speaking, to give honor and glory to Him, our one and only Sovereign—El Shaddai: God Almighty. Sometimes, we jump into prayer, immediately asking for what we need Him to do for us, like He is our personal vending machine. We act like little children making demands on their parent. Don't get me wrong. God loves us and wants us to come to Him and ask for what we need; He tells us to in Scripture. But Jesus's example of prayer demonstrates our need to acknowledge that He is God and He is Lord before we petition His help. Can you imagine storming into the oval office unannounced and demanding that the president of the United States hear your request? That will probably not end well for you. And he is just a man who has been given authority over this one nation. God is quite a bit above that!

"For as the heavens are higher than the earth, so are My ways higher than your ways and My thoughts than your thoughts" (Isaiah 55:9). He is God and has all authority in heaven and on earth. We should come before Him remembering that, honoring Him and giving Him the respect He is due, while also being totally cognizant of His deep and abiding love for us.

"Your kingdom come..."

Jesus came to set up His kingdom; and through His life, death, and resurrection, it was accomplished. "It is finished!" And there is still a kingdom to come—an eternal kingdom of perfect peace and perpetual praise to God. There's a great day coming! We need to be excited about that day! Maranatha! Come, Lord Jesus! Including this in our prayer life every day helps us to stay focused on what truly needs to be done each day. It helps us to think more about the lost souls around us and less about our own worldly problems. God wants everyone to be saved, and there are so many people who haven't heard the gospel or who have heard it but don't take it seriously. We have this great treasure—a kingdom relationship with God; and we need to share it with the world. Paul describes the kingdom as "righteousness, peace and joy in the Holy Spirit" (Romans 14:17). Everyone needs this great gift! The world longs for peace and joy, and they desperately need righteousness. This world is in dire need of a Savior. Every day of our life should be centered on this purpose. How can we advance God's kingdom on this earth today? It starts by spreading the word.

"Your will be done on earth as it is in heaven."

When we pray, it is often tempting to just ask for what we need or want without asking for God's will in the matter. There are even some Christian circles who say that submitting to God's will somehow shows a lack of faith, that praying for God's will gives Him an "out." Like if we pray with resolute faith, He has no other option but to do what we demand. They say we should pray with the highest confidence that we will receive whatever we ask. But while we are told in scripture to pray in faith without wavering, we are also told to submit to the will of God in our prayers. It means remembering and acknowledging that God is omnipotent—that He can do anything we ask, he has the power and the ability—while at the same time remembering that He also has the authority. He is *sovereign* and has the absolute right to say yes or no. Jesus, in the Garden of Gethsemane on the night before He was crucified, prayed earnestly that the suffering He was about to endure could be taken from Him; but He relinquished His will to the will of His Father. "Not what I will, but what you will" (Mark 14:36). What better example is there? Jesus Himself demonstrated this very important aspect of prayer. We pray in faith, believing that He is able to do what we are asking of Him; but we submit to His will so that whatever He chooses to do, we accept because He is God, He is Sovereign.

In Daniel 3:13, through the end of the chapter, we have the story of Shadrach, Meshach, and Abed-nego. The king of Babylon, Nebuchadnezzar, had made a golden image and commanded all the people that at the sound of the horn and music they should bow before the image and worship it. Because of their devotion to God, Shadrach, Meshach, and Abed-nego refused to bow down and were, therefore, sentenced to die in a fiery furnace. Nebuchadnezzar was furious with them and said, "What god is there who can deliver you out of my hands?" Here is their response:

> If it be so, our God whom we serve is able to deliver us from the furnace of blazing fire; and He will deliver us out of your hand, O king. But even if He does not, let it be known to you, O king, that we are not going to serve your gods or worship the golden image that you have set up. (Daniel 3:17–18)

Their answer is amazing! They totally honor God as their Deliverer, trusting Him completely—and they submit to His will, saying, "Even if He does not." Their devotion and obedience to God were stronger than their fear of death. They believed they would be delivered, either by life or by death. We know how the story ends— God sends His angel to join them in the furnace and protect them from harm. Many scholars and commentators say that this angel was the preincarnate Jesus Himself. He stood with them in the fire, and not one hair on their heads was singed. And He is with us when we go through the fire as well. Praying in faith, in full submission to His will is powerful! First John 5:14 states, "This is the confidence which we have before Him, that, if we ask anything according to His will, He hears us. And if we know that He hears us in whatever we ask, we know that we have the requests which we have asked from Him." Please note that this verse doesn't say He will give us whatever we ask but rather whatever we ask according to His will. We must keep Him on the throne and be willing to accept His answer, whether or not it's what we want, for His ways are perfect. For example, the apostle Paul, a man of strong faith in our Lord and who had the power to heal others, prayed that his thorn in the flesh would be removed from him; but God said no to his request. We don't know for sure what his thorn in the flesh was, but it was something that Paul struggled with. Some say it was his eyesight or some other physical malady; whatever it was, God saw fit to allow Paul to keep it.

> Therefore, in order to keep me from becoming conceited, I was given a thorn in my flesh, a messenger of Satan, to torment me. Three times I pleaded with the Lord to take it away from me. But he said to me, "My grace is sufficient for you, for my power is made perfect in weakness." Therefore I will boast all the more gladly about my weaknesses, so that Christ's power may rest on me. That is why, for Christ's sake, I delight in weaknesses, in insults, in hardships, in persecutions, in difficulties. For when I am weak, then I am strong. (2 Corinthians 12:7–10)

I love Paul's attitude here—let me be weak so that God's power may be upon me! Therefore, he became content in his struggles for Christ's sake. Note also that Paul's thorn in the flesh was given to him so that he would not become conceited. God knows what we need, even if we don't want to admit it to ourselves. He is omnipotent—all-powerful—and can do anything; this is what makes Him sovereign. He also knows better than we do what is best and how our request may affect others. We have to be willing to let Him be in control. Many times, I have heard people say that they gave up on God because they didn't get what they asked Him for. Often their request had to do with the healing of a loved one or the repair of a broken marriage…situations where their only hope was God, and He seemed to let them down. These are devastating and terribly difficult situations, to be sure. But we must believe that God is faithful, that He sees more than we do, and that He hurts right along with us. Jesus didn't remove Shadrach, Meshach, and Abed-nego from the fire; He stood with them in the fire. A day is coming when there will be no more death, no more corruption, and no more sorrow. We must look forward in hope to that day! Following the example of Paul, our attitude should also be in submission to His will in our lives. We pray, bringing our requests to the Father, but in humble and loving subjection to His will.

"Give us this day our daily bread…"

After acknowledging God's sovereignty and power, expressing a longing for His kingdom, and submitting to His will, then we bring our requests to Him. This puts our hearts in the proper position to petition Him. God wants to bless us. He wants to give us what we need. He encourages us to ask Him in faith, without doubting. God is a good Father, and He wants to help us. We can bring all of our cares, sorrows, desires, hopes, and dreams to Him. He sees every tear that we shed and hears the aching of our hearts when we cry out to Him. Jesus says, "Ask and it will be given to you" (Matthew 7:7). We are told to ask. He will answer us if our motives are pure and if He, in His divine wisdom, sees it to be beneficial for all involved.

Bring everything to the Lord. Ask Him for His will, His help, and His guidance. Plead with Him for healing. Petition Him on behalf of others in need. Whatever the need or request, take it to the Father and submit to His will, and He will take care of you. "The effective prayer of a righteous man can accomplish much" (James 5:16).

"And forgive us our debts as we have forgiven our debtors…"

To have a heart that acknowledges our need for a Savior is so important in building a faithful life. We need His mercy and forgiveness, and we have a responsibility to pass that mercy and forgiveness on to those who wrong us. It means letting go of the hurt feelings, the anger, or resentment—to metaphorically remove our hands from around their throat. Forgiveness frees us from being the judge and leaves that to God; it enables us to move on. Jesus teaches us to forgive seventy times seven. This is not to be taken literally but in a hyperbolic sense. It means to forgive all the time. Of course, it is easier to forgive a person if they are sorry for what they did. But we are to forgive always, even if the other person has no remorse for what they have done to us. Forgiveness does not mean that we are to allow people to walk all over us or abuse us or that there should be no consequence for their actions, but it is important to realize what it does mean. Forgiveness leaves the judgment to God and allows us to have peace within ourselves. It puts hatred and anger aside and allows God to fight for us. It is sometimes difficult to forgive someone who has wronged us, especially if that person was a close friend, spouse, or family member, when trust has been violated or when the hurt runs deep. But God understands and tells us to forgive. Forgiveness does not automatically rebuild trust, however. That takes time and, in some cases, may never fully return; but forgiveness frees us from the anger and resentment. Holding on to these things only weakens our faith and can eventually hinder our spiritual, physical, and emotional well-being. In Luke 6:37–38, Jesus says,

> Do not judge, and you will not be judged; and do
> not condemn, and you will not be condemned;

pardon, and you will be pardoned. Give, and it will be given to you. They will pour into your lap a good measure—pressed down, shaken together, and running over. For by your standard of measure it will be measured to you in return.

How we forgive is how we will be forgiven; how we judge, we will be judged. Occasionally, when some well-known Christian leader commits some egregious sin that becomes public, social media explodes with comments condemning the person to hell. And while that may or may not be the outcome for that individual, it is not our place to drop the gavel—it is God's. Therefore, we must be quick to forgive others so that God will be quick to forgive us. It doesn't mean we condone the actions or sinful behavior; it simply leaves judgment to God.

"Do not lead us into temptation, but deliver us from evil."

To pray for strength to overcome the temptations of each day is critical if we are going to be successful at it. Keeping that line of communication open is vital for conquering sin. If there is a specific temptation you are struggling with, speaking to God in the moment of temptation can steer you in the right direction. In Him, we are delivered from evil. Paul states in 2 Corinthians 10:5, "We are taking every thought captive to the obedience of Christ." So what does it mean to "take every thought captive"? It means that as soon as our mind starts to wander into temptation, we should check it. Grab that thought, and refuse to allow it to continue. Think immediately about something else. Steer our thoughts in a different direction. Talk to God or open the Bible and read. God is so good, and He wants us to lean on Him. He will help us; He will redirect our thoughts so that we don't fall into temptation. Our job is to be fully aware of when we are stepping into dangerous waters.

"For Thine is the kingdom and the power and glory forever. Amen."

This last phrase of the Lord's prayer was probably not part of Jesus's original prayer. The earliest manuscripts do not include it, so it seems probable that it was added later on. However, it makes for a very satisfying ending. To start a prayer with praise and adoration and to end it the same way seems very appropriate. All praise and glory belong to Him. Praying and spending time alone with God are vital parts of the Christian walk. But we also need and crave the worship and edification of the body of Christ, the church.

At the writing of this book, we are in the middle of COVID-19 lockdown. Our churches are not allowed to meet in person. Many churches, like the one we attend, are live-streaming services or having drive-in parking lot services; but it just isn't the same. I find myself longing for praise and worship with the family of God, to lift our voices together in song just can't be matched in a live stream. The longer this pandemic goes on, the more I ache in my soul for my church family.

Hebrews 10:24–25 states, "Let us consider how to stimulate one another to love and good deeds, not forsaking our own assembling together, as is the habit of some, but encouraging one another, and all the more as you see the day drawing near." Meeting together is meant to encourage us and to stimulate us to do good for others—to not lose hope but to keep pressing on. Without this love and encouragement, it's easy to get weighed down and discouraged.

Another example comes from Acts 9:31: "So the church throughout all Judea and Galilee and Samaria enjoyed peace, being built up; and going on in the fear of the Lord and in the comfort of the Holy Spirit, it continued to increase." To be built up and to go in the fear of the Lord and the comfort of the Holy Spirit—don't we all long for that? The body of Christ, the church, gives us this. We pray together, bringing our cares and concerns to God as a united body of believers. We sing songs of praise and worship, lifting our hands and voices together. We share at the Lord's *table* a communion, a remembrance of our Savior and His love and sacrifice for us. We hear a message from the Word of God to encourage and empower us. All these things lift us up and give us comfort in the Holy Spirit. It is possible to worship God through a live-streamed service or online; God is most definitely there with us. But there is something powerful about worshipping with other believers. You could compare it to a protest. You can protest online or in your own home watching it on TV, but it can't compare to hundreds of protesters getting together, live and in-person. It becomes something much different—something much more alive, powerful, and unrestrained. In similar fashion in the church, the Spirit moves through the body empowering every member. When I was younger, I spent many summers working at a Christian youth camp. One summer, as I was on kitchen duty, finishing up snack time and shutting down the main lodge area, I could hear the campers, down at the campfire, raising their voices in songs of praise and devotion—the sounds of their praise echoing through the trees. The Spirit within me longed to quit what I was doing and join in with the praise and worship. The Spirit yearns to participate with the family of God in joyful celebration of God's goodness. Oh, that we could be unrestrained in our worship!

Some people criticize the church and claim that "those people" are hypocritical and fake. They refuse to go to church, because they don't want to associate with fake, hypocritical people. But seriously, folks, aren't we all guilty here? Who among us doesn't put their best face forward when interacting with others? Don't we all try to hide our own ugliness? How many times have you thought you really knew someone, but they surprise you with an ugliness you never saw coming? This is not limited to the church—it's everywhere: at work, at school, even in our own homes, and among our own family members. Christians are not exempt from being human. This is the whole point: we *need* a Savior because without His grace, we are a mess—every single one of us. Being together with a group of people who are all striving to connect to God and live in relationship with Him is such an encouragement. Each one is looking to God, and together, we can lift each other up and help each other reach higher and higher. A. W. Tozer, in his book *The Pursuit of God: The Human Thirst for the Divine*, explains this with the analogy of a piano.

> Has it ever occurred to you that one hundred pianos all tuned to the same fork are automatically tuned to each other? They are of one accord by being tuned not to each other but to another standard to which each one must individually bow. So one hundred worshipers met together, each one looking away to Christ, are in heart nearer to each other than they could possibly be were they to become 'unity' conscious and turn their eyes away from God to strive for closer fellowship.[10]

What a beautiful picture of the body of Christ! Each of us in the family of God is looking to Him to find our perfect pitch. Because we each are tuned to a perfect God, we have unity with each other. Striving to unite the body without the anchor of a perfect God is pointless. It simply makes us self-focused instead of God-focused. To be truly united, we must all have the same focal point and be committed to our Sovereign God. So let me encourage you, if you want to be rooted and to grow in your faith, find a church home. Find one that is grounded in the word of God, that believes in the absolute truth of the Bible and isn't afraid to teach it.

The word of God is amazing! The more we study it and the more time we spend consuming it, the more deeply we will understand it. New insights are revealed, and connections we never saw before come to light with each new reading. "For the word of God is living and active and sharper than any two-edged sword" (Hebrews 4:12). If you've never read the entire Bible, it can seem like an overwhelming task. After all, it's a long book. But, in reality, it is sixty-six books, and they don't have to be read in order. The Old Testament, which relates the history of the Jewish people and the Law given

---

[10] A. W. Tozer, *The Pursuit of God: The Human Thirst for the Divine* (Bethany House, 2013).

under Moses, as well as the prophecies and promises of the coming Messiah, can be a bit more challenging to read. The New Testament is all about Jesus (actually, so is the Old Testament). His life, ministry, death, and resurrection are recorded in the Gospels—the first four books of the New Testament: Matthew, Mark, Luke, and John. The book of Acts relates the activities of the disciples of Jesus after He returns to heaven and how they continued to teach and spread the good news about Jesus. We are also introduced to Paul in the book of Acts. Much of the rest of the New Testament are letters written from Paul, Peter, and others to the new churches and Christians in the area, teaching them how to live the Christian life. The final book in the New Testament is Revelation, a vision received by John of hope and encouragement for Christians undergoing extreme persecution. It tells of the new heaven and the new earth. Of all the Gospel writers, John is my favorite. One of his main objectives was to portray the deity of Jesus Christ. If you've never read the Bible before, the Gospel of John is a great place to start.

For those of us who have read the Bible, it is easy to fall into complacency, thinking that "there's nothing new here." I encourage you to dig deeper! Buy some highlighters, and give each highlighter a different topic, and start reading, searching the scriptures for that specific topic. For example, in my Bible, the color purple represents the topic of the Trinity. Every time I come across a verse that relates to or supports this topic, I highlight it in purple. Before long, your Bible will be full of highlights, and you can quickly scan for a specific topic. Charles Spurgeon has several quotes about reading the Bible. Here are a couple of my favorites:

> Nobody ever outgrows Scripture; the book widens and deepens with our years.[11]
>
> Suppose a number of persons were to take it into their heads that they had to defend a lion, full-grown king of beasts! There he is in the cage,

---

[11] Charles Haddon Spurgeon, "The Talking Book," *Metropolitan Tabernacle Pulpit, Volume 17* (October 21, 1871), The Spurgeon Center, spurgeon.org.

and here come all the soldiers of the army to fight for him. Well, I should suggest to them, if they would not object, and feel that it was humbling to them, that they should kindly stand back, and open the door, and let the lion out! I believe that would be the best way of defending him, for he would take care of himself; and the best "apology" for the gospel is to let the gospel out.[12]

The Bible is the amazing Word of God. It is living and active. There are many other books in the world which, after reading them once, lose their draw. The first reading may have been enchanting and exciting, but subsequent readings just don't reach the same level of emotional engagement. But that is not true with the Bible. It grows with us. As we grow in our understanding of the Scriptures, new insights and understandings come to us. The Holy Spirit guides and encourages us as we read. We may have read the same passage many, many times in the past; but then one day it hits us in a brand-new way, touching us in a way it never had before, and we may find ourselves sobbing and convicted or touched by the love of God that floods from the pages. It speaks to us. It guides us. It interacts with us. This is why it is called living and active. There simply is no other book like that.

There are some who might try to persuade us that the Bible is not 100 percent accurate, that there are parts that just don't work for us in today's modern world. They try to manipulate the Word to fit their political or social worldview so that it will be more palatable, easier to swallow. This is dangerous ground. The word of God is inerrant. It is perfect and inspired by the Holy Spirit of God. Our God is amazing, omnipotent, and omniscient. He inspired His word to be complete and without error and to be passed down generation to generation in that perfect form. He is not so small and impotent

---

[12] Charles Haddon Spurgeon, "Christ and His Co-workers," volume 42, The Spurgeon Center (June 10, 1886), spurgeon.org. (Winger) (Browning) (Littauer) (Edwards, Sermon 12 on Charity: Willing to Undergo Sufferings for Christ.).

that He would create Scripture that would not pass the test of time. People who believe otherwise perhaps have too small a view of God. Be aware, though, that there are people who try to change the Word, who publish "translations" that are not true to the original text. We must be careful to not get sucked into false teachings—hold to what is true. Charles Spurgeon said it well in this quote from an 1871 sermon entitled *The Talking Book*.

> I am always sorry to be on bad terms with the Bible, for then I must be on bad terms with God. Whenever my creed does not square with God's word, I think it is time to [mold] my creed into another form. As for God's words, they must not be touched with hammer or axe. Oh, the [chiseling], and cutting, and hammering in certain commentaries to make God's Bible orthodox and systematic! How much better to leave it alone! The word is right, and we are wrong, wherein we agree not with it. The teachings of God's word are infallible, and must be reverenced as such. Now, when you love it so well that you would not touch a single line of it, and prize it so much that you would even die for the [defense] of one of its truths, then, as it is dear to you, you will be dear to it, and it will grasp you and unfold itself to you as it does not to the world.[13]

I love the line where Spurgeon says, "The word is right and we are wrong, wherein we agree not with it." Beautifully said! If we disagree with God's word, we are wrong, because His word is inerrant. We must love the word of God and reverence it, so much so that we would defend it with our very lives. How would we feel if we lost the advantage of having the Word? Would we be devastated? Or would

---

[13] Charles Haddon Spurgeon, "The Talking Book," *Metropolitan Tabernacle Pulpit*, volume 17, The Spurgeon Center (October 21, 1871), spurgeon.org.

we even notice its absence? We must keep the Word in our heart as a great treasure—worth everything we have to give.

Committing Scripture to memory is a great way to keep God's word in our heart. Many of us don't like this practice, because it can be difficult; it forces the brain to engage and think. However, this aids in understanding because we're not just reading quickly through the text. We read and reread and quote it back, and before long, it sticks. Then it is accessible, no matter where we are or what we are doing. Compare it to a young student who is trying to memorize their multiplication facts. By having these facts in their head, they are able to move through more difficult mathematical equations without stumbling over the basics. It's true in music as well. I practice scales, chords, and arpeggios so that when I am making music, I don't have to stop and figure out how to play that chord or which notes are sharp or flat. I can get lost in the music and go beyond the mechanics of it. It is the same way with our faith. Knowing the Bible is basic. Everything grows out of that understanding of the Spirit-inspired Scripture. So then, in the middle of the night or in the middle of a storm, we can recall, "The Lord is my Shepherd; I shall not want" (Psalm 23:1).

Finally, choose a good, solid translation when you're studying. There are many really good translations, as well as a few poor ones. My two favorites are the New American Standard Bible (NASB) and the New International Version (NIV). The NIV is a phrase for phrase translation, which means that the translators (a large group of people) took each phrase in the original languages and translated the phrase into English, not necessarily translating each individual word. This produces a translation that reads well and is easy to understand. The NASB is a word-for-word translation, which means that the translators (again, many of them) took each word in the original languages and translated it into English. This produces a very accurate translation, which is sometimes a bit more difficult to read, as the phraseology may not be as smooth in places. Choose a translation that was not done by a single individual or by a specific denomination, as there are no checks or balances for that type of translation. In my opinion, it is too easy for a single individual or denomination to incorporate their own biases and religious preferences into the text. For example, many cults who call themselves Christian have their own translations which have been altered from the original manuscripts to reflect their desired beliefs. Do not trust these translations. The NIV and NASB (as well as many other good translations) are translated by teams of people, hundreds of people from many different denominations, each checking and double-checking to be sure that the accuracy of the Scriptures is preserved. Do your research and choose a good, solid translation. Mike Winger, an associate pastor and teacher in Bellflower, California, has quite an extensive collection of YouTube videos on his channel, *Learn to Think Biblically*. In one of these videos entitled "Can I Trust Bible Translations?"[14] Mike goes into detail on several different translations explaining the positives and negatives of each. Mike is a great teacher, and I encourage you to subscribe to his channel and check out this video as well as hundreds of other videos on numerous topics. You can also find him on the internet at Biblethinker.org.

Spending time with God in prayer, Bible study, in worship and praise, both alone and with a church family, is how we grow roots. God's word is the mulch and fertilizer that enriches the soil of our hearts. Our relationship with Him gives us protection against all the environmental hazards the evil one can throw at us. We are safe from the wind, weather, and pests that Satan uses to get us off-course. The church offers us the support and encouragement that hold us up until our roots are strong, just as a stake holds up the young plant. We grow roots by being connected to the soil. A plant that has no root doesn't grow and is easily pulled up. A firmly rooted plant grips the soil and often, when pulled on, will break at the stem before giving up their grip on the soil, the source of life. We need to be so firmly rooted in God that we would rather suffer the loss of all things than to let go of Him. I have often heard it said that your roots are where you come from, but I disagree. Your roots are what you have

---

[14] Mike Winger, "Can I Trust Bible Translations?: Evidence for the Bible, part 17," *Learn to Think Biblically*, November 11, 2016, YouTube video.

anchored your life in. Anchor your life in what is eternal—in God alone.

> "Repent, and each of you be baptized in the name of Jesus Christ for the forgiveness of your sins; and you will receive the gift of the Holy Spirit. For the promise is for you and your children and for all who are far off, as many as the Lord our God will call to Himself." And with many other words he solemnly testified and kept on exhorting them, saying, "Be saved from this perverse generation!" So then, those who had received his word were baptized; and that day there were added about three thousand souls. They were continually devoting themselves to the apostles' teaching and to fellowship, to the breaking of bread and to prayer.
>
> Everyone kept feeling a sense of awe; and many wonders and signs were taking place through the apostles. And all those who had believed were together and had all things in common; and they began selling their property and possessions and were sharing them with all, as anyone might have need. Day by day continuing with one mind in the temple, and breaking bread from house to house, they were taking their meals together with gladness and sincerity of heart, praising God and having favor with all the people. And the Lord was adding to their number day by day those who were being saved. (Acts 2:38–47)

Questions to Consider

Chapter 3: The Root

1. There is a poem by Elizabeth Barrett Browning called "How Do I Love Thee? Let Me Count the Ways."[15] List your top ten reasons for loving God (Use extra paper, if needed).

_____

_____

_____

_____

_____

_____

_____

2. On a scale of 1 to 10, with 1 being not at all important and 10 being the most important thing in your life, how important is daily prayer in your life? How successful are you at praying without ceasing?

   1   2   3   4   5   6   7   8   9   10

3. On a scale of 1 to 10, with 1 being not at all important and 10 being the most important thing in your life, how important is daily Bible study in your life?

   1   2   3   4   5   6   7   8   9   10

4. On a scale of 1 to 10, with 1 being not at all and 10 being absolutely, no question, do you believe that the Bible is the inerrant Word of God?

   1   2   3   4   5   6   7   8   9   10

---

[15] Elizabeth Barrett Browning, "How Do I Love Thee? (Sonnet 43)," Public Domain.

Using the lines below, write out Colossians 2:6–7. Reread it many times during the week. Try to commit it to memory.

_____

_____
_____
_____
_____
_____
_____
_____
_____
_____
_____
_____
_____
_____
_____
_____
_____
_____
_____
_____
_____
_____
_____
_____
_____
_____

Our God and Father, thank You for being our God, for Your Sovereignty and might. Teach us to love You more, to love Your word, and to follow You with all of our heart. We love You, Lord! In Jesus's name, amen.

CHAPTER 4

Pruning

The vinedresser is never nearer the branches
than when he is pruning them.[16]

—David Jeremiah

The purpose of pruning is to improve the quality of the roses,
not to hurt the bush.[17]

—Florence Littauer

I am the true vine and My Father is the vinedresser. Every branch
in Me that does not bear fruit, He takes away; and every branch
that bears fruit, He prunes it so that it may bear more fruit.

—John 15:1–2

Pruning is a necessary part of gardening. It is essential for the maximum health and future harvest of the plants and trees we choose to grow. It may seem harsh or even counterintuitive to cut back in order to flourish, but it is the best way to insure a healthy crop. While the jalapeño plants are still small, we pull any blossoms off, forcing nutrients into the developing roots and branches, causing increased growth. The tiny plant has blossoms and will produce peppers but may not be strong enough to support them. A large and strong plant

---

[16] Dr. David Jeremiah is the senior pastor of Shadow Mountain Community Church in El Cajon, California, author of many books and the host of "Turning Point," a radio ministry that is heard around the world.

[17] Florence Littauer, *It Takes So Little to be Above Average* (Harvest House Publishers, 1996), 63.

will produce more quantity and better-quality peppers in the long run than a tiny, scrawny plant.

In our garden, we have several rows of raspberry plants. These plants produce berries twice a year, in late spring and again in late summer or early fall. In the late spring, raspberries are harvested. After which, the canes that bore the fruit die off, and new canes come up from the roots. Pruning back the old canes increases the energy flowing into the new canes, insuring a great and bountiful harvest in the fall, when the new canes will bear fruit. Or take fruit trees for example. As a tree grows, occasionally branches may die off or become damaged by wind and weather. A damaged or dead branch will continue to draw nutrients from the tree, as the tree attempts to heal itself. Because of this drain of energy, the rest of the tree struggles to thrive. By cutting away the dead or damaged branches, 100 percent of the tree's energy can be directed toward the healthy branches and the developing fruit. In this way, pruning is actually helping the harvest to be more bountiful with better-developed fruit.

Pruning can be difficult. Sometimes, we have to severely cut a plant back in order to save it. We have several rose bushes in our garden. Recently, one of our lovely red roses developed a bad case of black spot. Black spot is a disease that affects roses, showing up as ugly black blotches on the leaves, which eventually dry up and fall off. Extremely prevalent in our moist Pacific Northwest climate, this disease weakens the plants and can contribute to their death. To cure black spot, we have to remove any leaf, stem, and blossom that have spots on them and dispose of them, even making sure there are no stray leaves on the ground, as the fungus can live for a long time on the dead leaves. Only after removing the black-spotted leaves could we then effectively treat the plant with medicated sprays and systemic remedies. But there were so many affected leaves and stems! Often, black spot can quickly take over a plant, affecting nearly every visible leaf and blossom. What was left after this harsh pruning was little more than a stick or two coming out of the ground. It broke my heart to see my pretty rose in such a state. But it wasn't long after this treatment that we could see sprouts coming out of the seemingly dead branches, and within a few weeks, new spot-free leaves opened up. Soon after, we had beautiful red roses blooming! What seemed at the moment to be destructive turned out to be beneficial in the long run.

Weeding the soil is another necessary chore in the garden. Like pruning, weeding helps the cultivated plants to grow stronger. Weeds are wild plants growing where they are not wanted that compete with cultivated plants. They steal the nutrients from the soil, and the garden plants suffer. It seems that weeds are able to grow just about anywhere. They can be invasive and take over the garden in no time, killing the cultivated plants by sucking up all the goodness in the soil. By removing the weeds, the garden plants are able to thrive and produce more fruit.

God is the Master Gardener. He has planted His word in our hearts and given us His precious Spirit to increase our growth. As we grow to maturity in our faith, sometimes we need a bit of pruning, to guide us and to keep us on track. He also removes the weeds that distract us from His purposes. What does it mean to be pruned by God? In John 15, Jesus uses the metaphor of a grape vine, where He is the vine and we are the branches. God is the Gardener Who prunes the vines.

> I am the true vine, and My Father is the vine-dresser. Every branch in Me that does not bear fruit, He takes away; and every branch that bears fruit, He prunes it so that it may bear more fruit. You are already clean because of the word which I have spoken to you. Abide in Me, and I in you. As the branch cannot bear fruit of itself unless it abides in the vine, so neither can you unless you abide in Me. I am the vine, you are the branches; he who abides in Me and I in him, he bears much fruit, for apart from Me you can do nothing. If anyone does not abide in Me, he is thrown away as a branch and dries up; and they gather them, and cast them into the fire and they are burned. If you abide in Me, and My words abide in you,

ask whatever you wish, and it will be done for you. My Father is glorified by this, that you bear much fruit, and so prove to be My disciples. Just as the Father has loved Me, I have also loved you; abide in My love. If you keep My commandments, you will abide in My love; just as I have kept My Father's commandments and abide in His love. These things I have spoken to you so that My joy may be in you, and that your joy may be made full. (John 15:1–11)

Grapes and vineyards were a common crop in the areas where Jesus had His ministry. I imagine they covered many hillsides in and around Galilee and Judea, so they made for a great visual aid as Jesus taught. Grapes grow from a strong main vine, which is the strength and heart of the plant. Branches sprout forth from the main vine and wrap around the posts and guidewires. These meandering branches get thinner and more fragile the farther from the vine they get. The thin, weak branches cannot bear the weight of the heavy bunches of grapes, and the fruit can wind up in the dirt. Pruning the weak and scrawny ends strengthens the branch and better supports the heavy clusters of sweet grapes that will soon form. Pruning is God's way of removing from our hearts anything that is hindering us from being firmly attached to Him, as the branches are attached to the vine. This is a positive thing, for don't we all want to be completely surrendered to His will—to remove from our lives anything that resembles evil? It is good that God is purifying us and working on us to cut away what is dead or dying. This makes us more fruitful and useful to Him. God wants us to be fruitful, and He will work on us to cultivate our faith and make us more beautiful and productive in His kingdom. He wants us to spread His love to the world. Just as with the grape vine, the farther away from the vine we get, the weaker we become, and the less apt we are to bear fruit. The passage in John 15 is very clear. A branch that does not bear fruit is cut away and thrown in the fire. If we are abiding in Him, we will bear fruit. It is only natural. Verse 8 says that the Father is glorified when we bear fruit and so prove to be His disciples. If we are not bearing fruit, are we truly His disciples?

Within this passage, there is also a promise that if we are abiding in Him and bearing fruit, whatever we ask will be done for us. Now I don't think this means that He will give us the winning lottery numbers or make someone fall in love with us. That's not what He's talking about. He's talking about bearing fruit. If we ask God for a deeper understanding of His word so we can teach others the Gospel, He will most assuredly do it. If we ask Him to lead us to someone who needs His love in their lives, know that He wants this too. If our heart is His and we are concerned for His kingdom, whatever we ask Him, He will do so that we can bear fruit. Jesus told his disciples that they could ask the Father for anything, and He would grant it so that they could bear fruit. In Acts 4, Peter and the other followers of Jesus are gathered together praying. They ask God that they would be able to speak His word courageously, and He answered them immediately.

> "For truly in this city there were gathered together against Your holy servant Jesus, whom You anointed, both Herod and Pontius Pilate, along with the Gentiles and the peoples of Israel, to do whatever Your hand and Your purpose predestined to occur. And now, Lord, take note of their threats, and grant that Your bond-servants may speak Your word with all confidence, while You extend Your hand to heal, and signs and wonders take place through the name of Your holy servant Jesus." And when they had prayed, the place where they had gathered together was shaken, and they were all filled with the Holy Spirit and began to speak the word of God with boldness. (Acts 4:27–31)

God immediately granted their request with a powerful outpouring of the Holy Spirit, giving them boldness and courage, with the outcome being that they spoke the word of God boldly. God's word was preached, and the Father was glorified.

Our joy is made full when we are abiding in Him and bearing fruit for Him, but we know that pruning will come, and this is not always easy. It is inevitable for all of us that hard times will come. However, James says, "Consider it all joy, my brethren, when you encounter various trials, knowing that the testing of your faith produces endurance. And let endurance have its perfect result, so that you may be perfect and complete, lacking in nothing" (James 1:2–4). Difficult times test our faith. When we go through trials, we learn to endure and lean on God. Our trials and periods of testing are God's way of pruning us. Difficult times most assuredly will come; everyone encounters them. Through faith, we can get through them. So even though we may be going through difficult times when God is pruning us, we have joy because we know that God is making us stronger and better equipped to bear fruit.

There are trials and troubles that we have no control over—that come upon us even though we have been faithful. At other times, we bring trials and trouble into our lives by following our fleshly nature rather than the Spirit. When we believe in Him, when we accept Him as our Lord and Savior, our sins are washed away; we are baptized into His family and are pure and undefiled in His sight, and His Holy Spirit dwells within us. But does this mean we are no longer influenced by the world, that our sinful nature will never take hold of us again? Not hardly. Paul dealt with this same issue in his letter to the Romans.

> For I know that nothing good dwells in me, that is, in my flesh; for the willing is present in me, but the doing of the good is not. For the good that I want, I do not do, but I practice the very evil that I do not want. But if I am doing the very thing I do not want, I am no longer the one doing it, but sin which dwells in me.
>
> I find then the principle that evil is present in me, the one who wants to do good. For I

> joyfully concur with the law of God in the inner man, but I see a different law in the members of my body, waging war against the law of my mind and making me a prisoner of the law of sin which is in my members. Wretched man that I am! Who will set me free from the body of this death? Thanks be to God through Jesus Christ our Lord! So then, on the one hand I myself with my mind am serving the law of God, but on the other, with my flesh the law of sin.
>
> Therefore there is now no condemnation for those who are in Christ Jesus. For the law of the Spirit of life in Christ Jesus has set you free from the law of sin and of death. (Romans 7:18–8:2)

We will continue to fight against sin for as long as we live, until we are set free from this body. But we do not fight this battle alone; God Himself indwells us and gives us a stronghold in which to anchor our souls. For if we have the Spirit of God in us, we can continue to put to death the fleshly nature, for He gives us the power to do so. In Romans 8:13, Paul continues, "For if you are living according to the flesh, you must die; but if by the Spirit, you are putting to death the deeds of the body, you will live." The Spirit of God within us helps us to fight against the sin that runs rampant in this world and enables us to live a godly and holy life in Him.

Suffering, trials, and tribulations are an inevitable part of life. We were never promised a life free from pain or sorrow. James said, "Consider it all joy, my brethren WHEN you encounter various trials" (James 1:2; emphasis mine). He did not say "if" you do but "when" you do. God says a similar thing in Isaiah 43:2. "When you pass through the waters, I will be with you; and through the rivers, they will not overflow you. When you walk through the fire, you will not be scorched, nor will the flame burn you." Times of struggle, pain, and suffering will come; but we do not go through it alone. He is with us because we are His children. We suffer with Him so that we may also receive glory with Him.

> The Spirit Himself testifies with our spirit that we are children of God, and if children, heirs also, heirs of God and fellow heirs with Christ, if indeed we suffer with Him so that we may also be glorified with Him. (Romans 8:16–17)

When we go through trials, our fleshly nature has a tendency to rear up. It is so very hard to mask it when we are struggling, angry, depressed, or overwhelmed. This is God's way of pruning us. He exposes the ugly parts and makes us aware of them, like a gardener lifts the healthy branches out of the way to reveal the dead and dying ones hiding under the surface. Then we can focus our attention on ridding ourselves of these fleshly behaviors and attitudes, with the help of the Holy Spirit.

"Pruning" can come in many forms: delayed answers to fervent prayer, struggles with coworkers or family members, everyday frustrations, pain, sickness… The list is endless. Everyone has struggles in this life, and our struggles may reveal the ugliness that is hiding underneath: our lack of faith, compassion, patience, or tolerance. In fact, many times it is the smallest, most petty struggles that frustrate us the most: traffic, running late, lost keys, barking dogs, spilled coffee, unfinished chores, cranky coworkers or family members, interruptions, constant noise… These small, seemingly innocuous stressors can bring out an attitude in us that we prefer no one would ever see: impatience, intolerance, anger, bad language, and other out-of-control behaviors. But God brings these to the surface to show us what we are hiding—to help us "weed them out." If we can readjust our thoughts and realize that these petty trials are actually drawing us closer to God, then we can "count it all joy."

So what about the big struggles: cancer or other serious illness, death of a loved one, loss of a home or a job, divorce, abuse—desperate prayers that seemingly go unheard or unanswered? Are these, too, a "pruning" from God? The answer is *no* and *yes*. I don't believe that God causes cancer or wills a person's child to die. I see Him as far too loving and merciful to be so callous. He is God and has the absolute right to do whatever He pleases. He is Sovereign and Lord over all; but we also live in a fallen world, where Satan has power, and I believe that the evil one is working to destroy our faith. Everything in this world is dying and fading away. The world itself is in bondage to decay and corruption. Paul continues in Romans 8:19–21:

> For the anxious longing of the creation waits eagerly for the revealing of the sons of God. For the creation was subjected to futility, not willingly, but because of Him who subjected it, in hope that the creation itself also will be set free from its slavery to corruption into the freedom of the glory of the children of God.

This world is not perfect. Death, sickness, and loss are a part of this world; and God loves us dearly and is always close to us when we are hurting. With God's help and the guidance of the Spirit, we can persevere through these difficult times, as we also long to be set free from the corruption of this world. Jonathan Edwards, an American revivalist preacher, lived and preached during the 1700s; and still his message rings true. This excerpt is from his twelfth sermon on charity, *Willing to Undergo All Sufferings for Christ*.

> They that are truly Christians, have that faith whereby they see that which is more than sufficient to make up for the greatest sufferings they can endure in the cause of Christ.—They see that excellency in God and Christ, whom they have chosen for their portion, which far outweighs all possible sufferings. And they see, too, that glory which God has promised to them that suffer for his sake—that far more exceeding and eternal weight of glory which their sufferings for Christ's sake work out for them, and in comparison with

which, the heaviest sorrows and most enduring trials are but "light affliction, which is but for a moment."

It is the character of true Christians, that they overcome the world.—"Whatsoever is born of God overcometh the world" (1 John 5:4). But to overcome the world, implies that we overcome alike its flatteries and frowns, its sufferings and difficulties. These are the weapons of the world, by which it seeks to conquer us; and if there be any of these that we have not a spirit to encounter for Christ's sake, then by such weapons the world will have us in subjection, and gain the victory over us. But Christ gives his servants the victory over the world in all its forms. They are conquerors, and more than conquerors, through him that hath loved them.[18]

Edwards reminds us that Satan will use our struggles, hardships, and sorrows to get the upper hand and lure us away from God. As the branches suffer through the pruning process and as a result a stronger, more fruitful branch develops; so we endure and persevere through our trials, to gain the victory in Jesus Christ. In this, we can have hope that even though what we are going through may be incredibly difficult, at the end of the tunnel is the Light of the World. We can look ahead to an "eternal weight of glory," to focus on the things which are eternal and look past the things of this world.

For momentary, light affliction is producing for us an eternal weight of glory far beyond all comparison, while we look not at the things which are seen, but at the things which are not seen; for the things which are seen are temporal, but

---

[18] Jonathan Edwards, "Sermon 12 on Charity: Willing to Undergo all Sufferings for Christ," A Puritan's Mind, apuritansmind.com, © 1996–2021.

the things which are not seen are eternal. (2
Corinthians 4:17–18)

In the Old Testament, we read about the life of Job, a faithful servant of God. God allowed Satan to take everything from him except his life. Satan believed he could destroy Job's faith, that Job would curse God and die, but he never did. Even though he had lost everything and was afflicted physically, even though his friends believed he was sinful and was receiving justice from God, Job remained faithful. He was like that plant, so firmly rooted that it would sacrifice the leaves, branches, stalks, and everything else above the ground rather than release its grip on the soil. And in the end, God blessed Job and restored to him over and above what he had previously.

God uses the big struggles to strengthen us and to increase our faith. But he takes no pleasure in our sorrow and grief. He is near to the brokenhearted, and He sees every tear that we cry. In struggles, in pain, in sickness, and eventually in death, He is with us. He will never leave us. He is leading us to His eternal home, where there will be no more sorrow or sickness or suffering, where pain and death will be no more. What a glorious day that will be! We look forward to this eternal home, which He has prepared for those who love Him. But there are many people who don't know Him and who need Him in their lives. God prunes us and nurtures us for one purpose: that we can bear fruit and draw the lost to Him.

Questions to Consider

Chapter 4: Pruning

1. What does it mean to be a part of the vine?

   _____
   _____
   _____
   _____
   _____

2. According to John 15:1–11, God will do for us whatever we ask on what condition?

   _____
   _____
   _____
   _____
   _____

3. In what ways has God "pruned" you? In what ways did this pruning benefit you?

   _____
   _____
   _____
   _____
   _____

4. In your opinion, how do you distinguish between God's pruning and Satan's schemes?

   _____
   _____
   _____
   _____

Using the lines below, write out John 15:1–2. Reread it many times during the week. Try to commit it to memory.

_____
_____
_____
_____
_____
_____
_____
_____
_____
_____
_____
_____
_____
_____
_____
_____
_____
_____
_____
_____
_____
_____
_____
_____

Father,

Thank You for being our Root and Foundation. Help us to be submissive to Your will and your "pruning" in our lives. Give us wisdom and discernment.
In Jesus's name, amen.

PART 2

Bear Fruit

CHAPTER 5

Bear Fruit

Is it a fast like this which I choose, a day
for a man to humble himself?
Is it for bowing one's head like a reed
and for spreading out sackcloth and ashes as a bed?
Will you call this a fast, even an acceptable day to the LORD?
Is this not the fast which I choose, to
loosen the bonds of wickedness,
to undo the bands of the yoke, and to let the oppressed go free
and break every yoke?
Is it not to divide your bread with the hungry
and bring the homeless poor into the house;
when you see the naked, to cover him;
and not to hide yourself from your own flesh?
Then your light will break out like the dawn, and your recovery will
speedily spring forth; and your righteousness will go before you;
the glory of the LORD will be your rear guard.
Then you will call, and the LORD will answer;
you will cry, and He will say, "Here I am."
If you remove the yoke from your midst, the pointing of the finger
and speaking wickedness, and if you give yourself to the hungry
and satisfy the desire of the afflicted, then your light will rise
in darkness and your gloom will become like midday.
And the LORD will continually guide you,
and satisfy your desire in scorched places,
and give strength to your bones;

and you will be like a watered garden,
and like a spring of water whose waters do not fail.
—Isaiah 58:1–11

God be gracious to us and bless us,
And cause His face to shine upon us—Selah.
That Your way may be known on the earth,
Your salvation among all nations.
Let the peoples praise You, O God; Let all the peoples praise You.
Let the nations be glad and sing for joy;
For You will judge the peoples with uprightness
And guide the nations on the earth. Selah.
Let the peoples praise You, O God; Let all the peoples praise You.
The earth has yielded its produce;
God, our God, blesses us. God blesses us,
That all the ends of the earth may fear Him.
—Psalm 67

Summer is such a wonderful season! Warming the ground, the sun encourages the roots to grow even deeper, reaching for the moisture and nutrients deep in the soil. The plants are growing and blooming, and soon tiny fruits and vegetables can be seen. Every day is exciting to see how much the fruit has grown overnight, eagerly awaiting the harvest. Different types of fruits or vegetables require a different length of time for full maturity of the produce. For example, radishes grow rather quickly and can be harvested and replanted several times in a summer. Pumpkins, on the other hand, take all summer and into the fall before they are done growing and turn a brilliant shade of orange. For some plants, the harvest is ongoing, throughout the summer. If anyone has planted zucchini, you have probably experienced this. These plants produce fruit so quickly, I'd bet if you watched closely for even a few minutes, you could witness the growth. I don't know how many times we've seen a tiny baby squash on the vine and then the next day it's the size of a football! They produce so many zucchinis it's hard to keep up with them. Other plants require years of growth before they are ready to produce. Fruit trees, for example, don't bear fruit for the first several years until the tree has had time to grow and develop strong roots and branches. Asparagus also needs several years before we can harvest the tender sprouts. If we try to harvest the sprouts before the root system is established, we can kill the plants. However, once established, we can enjoy this delicious sprout for decades to come.

Summer is a time for gathering fruits, vegetables, herbs, and flowers, enjoying their freshness in the moment and canning and preserving some for the winter months. In similar fashion, once we are rooted in God's love and grounded in His truth, we will bear fruit. It's not a matter of "if" we will but "when" we will. If the Spirit of God lives in us, the natural result is a fruitful life. His Spirit within us will motivate and encourage us to reach out to others, to comfort the brokenhearted, to help the sick and needy, to give encouragement to the struggling, or to simply bring a bit of joy to someone's day. The Spirit may also guide you to a soul who desperately needs Him. Whatever the Spirit calls us to do, we should do it with all our heart.

The Spirit leads us to bear fruit for God, but what is the fruit that we bear? Is it the people you interact with who come to know Him, or is it the actions you take as you follow the Spirit's leading? The answer is both, and they are obviously very closely related. Just as in the garden, there are many different types of plants, so it is in the body of Christ. Each of us has gifts that God has given us to be used in His service. Together, with the help of the Spirit, we work to build up and expand the body of Christ. In Galatians 5, Paul is encouraging us to walk by the Spirit, not by the flesh. The fruits of the Spirit are the gifts that the Spirit will bring to fruition when we submit to Him. "But the fruit of the Spirit is love, joy, peace, patience, kindness, goodness, faithfulness, gentleness, self-control; against such things there is no law" (Galatians 5:22–23). These character traits are gifts of the Spirit, given to those who believe. Although they may not be fully developed and mature, the seeds of these fruits, given through the Spirit, will—through faith, perseverance, and the leading of the Spirit—come to full maturity. Dietrich Bonhoeffer, a Lutheran pastor and theologian during the 1930s and 1940s, wrote a powerful book entitled *The Cost of Discipleship*, in which he comments on these miraculous gifts of the Spirit.

> Fruit is always the miraculous, the created; it is never the result of willing but always a growth. The fruit of the Spirit is a gift of God, and only He can produce it. They who bear it know as little about it as the tree knows of its fruit. They know only the power of Him on whom their life depends.[19]

The Spirit gives these amazing character traits to all of us who believe and have surrendered our lives to Jesus. These attributes are present to some extent in all of us making a claim to godliness because the Spirit of God abides in us. If we are lacking in any of these areas, it is important that we examine our hearts to see if we are, in some way, putting out the Spirit's fire within us. The Spirit will point out our areas of weakness and encourage us to overcome. As we discussed previously, God may use trials and struggles to strengthen certain areas of our faith, much like a gardener who prunes back a plant, removing dead leaves and branches, to enable the plant to grow stronger in the long run. As was mentioned previously, I don't believe that God causes sickness and pain, in the same way that the gardener doesn't cause his plants to become diseased. Satan is the cause of pain, suffering, and death. God works in these situations to bring us through our trials stronger and more deeply connected to Him.

Living a life led by the Spirit means living unselfishly, putting others ahead of ourselves. Our culture teaches a concept that is totally counter to this. Society tells us that we have to take care of our own needs first. As a culture, we are often unable to see beyond our own bubble. This trend in society has been called the "Me Generation."

> The "Me Generation" in the United States is a term referring to the baby boomer generation and the

---

[19] Dietrich Bonhoeffer, *The Cost of Discipleship* (United States: Touchstone, 2012), 285.

self-involved qualities that some people associated with it. The baby boomers (Americans born during the 1946–1964 baby boom) were dubbed the "Me" generation by writer Tom Wolfe during the 1970s; Christopher Lasch was another writer who commented on the rise of a culture of narcissism among the younger generation. The phrase caught on with the general public at a time when "self-realization" and "self-fulfillment" were becoming cultural aspirations to which young people supposedly ascribed higher importance than social responsibility.[20]

This type of thinking generates a society that is primarily concerned with self. "What is in it for me?" becomes a first response. Doing acts that are for the good of society or are motivated purely by love are disappearing, unless there is some benefit to self. True philanthropy is a rare thing in this type of society. Unfortunately, it hasn't gotten better over the years. The children of baby boomers, the millennials, are reportedly even more self-absorbed. Joel Stein, a writer for *Time* magazine, dubbed them the "Me Me Me generation."

The incidence of narcissistic personality disorder is nearly three times as high for people in their 20s as for the generation that's now 65 or older, according to the National Institutes of Health; 58% more college students scored higher on a narcissism scale in 2009 than in 1982.[21]

When self-absorbed people raise self-absorbed children, we wind up with a whole new generation of narcissistic people. We have raised a generation who are never told no, who are rewarded regardless of their effort, who have little to no work ethic but expect to

[20] Neal Patrick, "The Baby Boomers Were Nicknamed the 'Me Generation' Due to Their Perceived Narcissism," *The Vintage News*, September 5, 2016.
[21] Joel Stein, "The Me Me Me Generation," *Time Magazine*, May 20, 2013.

receive the benefits as if they had. Narcissism is a serious problem in today's world. The word is Greek in its origin and stems from the mythology of a man named Narcissus, who was so obsessed with his own image that he eventually died of starvation because he couldn't pull himself away from his own reflection even to eat. Many people today are caught up in this self-absorbed state of mind. The Mayo Clinic lists several symptoms of narcissistic personality disorder, which are quite interesting and familiar in our society.

> Narcissistic personality disorder—one of several types of personality disorders—is a mental condition in which people have an inflated sense of their own importance, a deep need for excessive attention and admiration, troubled relationships, and a lack of empathy for others. But behind this mask of extreme confidence lies a fragile self-esteem that's vulnerable to the slightest criticism.
> Signs and symptoms of narcissistic personality disorder and the severity of symptoms vary. People with the disorder can
>
> - Have an exaggerated sense of self-importance;
> - Have a sense of entitlement and require constant, excessive admiration;
> - Expect to be recognized as superior even without achievements that warrant it;
> - Exaggerate achievements and talents
> - Be preoccupied with fantasies about success, power, brilliance, beauty, or the perfect mate;
> - Believe they are superior and can only associate with equally special people;
> - Monopolize conversations and belittle or look down on people they perceive as inferior;
> - Expect special favors and unquestioning compliance with their expectations;

- Take advantage of others to get what they want;
- Have an inability or unwillingness to recognize the needs and feelings of others;
- Be envious of others and believe others envy them;
- Behave in an arrogant or haughty manner, coming across as conceited, boastful, and pretentious; and
- Insist on having the best of everything—for instance, the best car or office.
- At the same time, people with narcissistic personality disorder have trouble handling anything they perceive as criticism, and they can
- Become impatient or angry when they don't receive special treatment;
- Have significant interpersonal problems and easily feel slighted;
- React with rage or contempt and try to belittle the other person to make themselves appear superior;
- Have difficulty regulating emotions and behavior;
- Experience major problems dealing with stress and adapting to change;
- Feel depressed and moody because they fall short of perfection; and
- Have secret feelings of insecurity, shame, vulnerability, and humiliation.[22]

Does any of this sound familiar to you? Narcissism is running rampant in our world today. Our culture encourages it through tele-

---

[22] Mayo Clinic Staff, "Narcissistic Personality Disorder," Mayo Foundation for Medical Education and Research (MFMER).

vision, movies, and social media. "Selfies" are plastered all over social media. "Here's me doing this...," "Here's me doing that...," "Here's what I'm eating for dinner...," "Here's me at work...," "Here's me at home...," "Here's me with my cat..." It goes on and on. Our culture teaches us to take care of ourselves and our needs first. The needs of self overrule the needs of anyone else around us. We see this in many different aspects of society in the way we interact with the people around us. It is a very self-centered and selfish attitude. Society tells us that self-esteem is the most important thing, to the extent that one can never be disagreed with or corrected, because it might damage their self-esteem. It creates a community where we blame everyone else for our problems and refuse to see our own flaws. It raises up people who have no need for Jesus, because they do not believe they are sinners; they are plenty righteous without Him. John MacArthur—a pastor-teacher at Grace Community Church in Sun Valley, California, and a featured teacher with the Grace to You media ministry—put it this way: "The self-esteem cult that goes around saying we've got to build up people's self-esteem is taking them the opposite way than the message of the Bible does because the more you love yourself, the less likely you are to need a Savior."[23] This creates people who are totally self-absorbed. We are trained to see only how something affects us personally. Reluctant to give up our own comfort for the sake of someone else, we hoard the blessings God has given us. But this is not what God has called us to. It's not what we were created for. Have you ever seen a narcissistic plant? A plant that is completely self-absorbed? No. A plant's purpose is to grow and produce fruit or seeds that provide food, shelter, and oxygen for the inhabitants of the earth. They provide shade and beauty and reproduce so that the next generation of plants can continue to do the same. A plant that refuses its purpose dies or is pulled up by the gardener. A. W. Tozer, in his book *The Pursuit of God: The Human Thirst for the Divine*, comments on this same analogy of plants and roots, as it relates to self-absorption and hoarding our blessings, interestingly written many years before

---

[23] John MacArthur, "Winning by Losing: The Paradox of Discipleship," Sermon #2321, Grace to You, October 24, 1982, gty.org, © 2021.

the "Me Generation." Apparently, this problem of self-absorption has been around for a long time, as far back as the garden of Eden.

> There is within the human heart a tough fibrous root of fallen life whose nature is to possess, always to possess. It covets "things" with a deep and fierce passion. The pronouns "my" and "mine" look innocent enough in print, but their constant and universal use is significant. They express the real nature of the old Adamic man better than a thousand volumes of theology could do. They are verbal symptoms of our deep disease. The roots of our hearts have grown down into things, and we dare not pull up one rootlet lest we die. Things have become necessary to us, a development never originally intended. God's gifts now take the place of God, and the whole course of nature is upset by the monstrous substitution.[24]

If we want to be led by the Spirit, we have to get outside ourselves and consider how to bless the lives of others. We have to be willing to put the needs of others ahead of our own needs. If we, as a society, could do this, there would be an end to many of the problems we face in today's world. Imagine how this attitude of self-sacrifice might affect homelessness, hunger, murder rates, corruption, abortion, hatred, racism… It could transform the world! Jesus calls us to this. Just as the branches bear fruit when attached to the vine, so we will bear fruit when attached to Jesus Christ. His Spirit is within us and gives us His character. The fruits of the Spirit—love, joy, peace, patience, kindness, goodness, faithfulness, gentleness, and self-control—are a gift from the Spirit to guide us to becoming less and less self-absorbed and more and more Spirit-absorbed. In the next sections, we will look closely at each of these gifts of the Spirit.

---

[24] A. W. Tozer, *The Pursuit of God: The Human Thirst for the Divine* (Project Gutenberg e-book, 2008, first published in 1948, Public domain in the USA), 22.

Questions to Consider

Chapter 5: Bear Fruit

1. What does it mean to bear fruit for God?

_____

_____

_____

_____

_____

2. List the fruits of the Spirit.

_____

_____

_____

_____

_____

3. How do we receive the gifts of the Spirit?

_____

_____

_____

_____

_____

4. What is narcissism?

_____

_____

_____

_____

5. How does narcissistic behavior affect the fruits of the Spirit?

_____

_____

_____

_____

_____

Using the lines below, write out Galatians 5:22–23. Reread it many times during the week. Try to commit it to memory.

_____
_____
_____
_____
_____
_____
_____
_____
_____
_____
_____
_____
_____
_____
_____
_____
_____
_____
_____
_____
_____
_____
_____
_____
_____

Holy God,

Thank You for the gift of Your Holy Spirit and the fruits of Your Spirit, which help us to live a godly life. Help us to see beyond our own desires and focus on the needs of others. In Jesus's name, amen.

CHAPTER 6

Love

Beyond all these things put on love, which
is the perfect bond of unity.
—Colossians 3:14

To have found God and still to pursue Him
is the soul's paradox of love.[25]
—A. W. Tozer

All the fruits of the Spirit which we are to lay weight
upon as evidential of grace, are summed up in charity, or
Christian love; because this is the sum of all grace.
And the only way, therefore, in which any
can know their good estate,
is by discerning the exercises of this divine charity in their hearts;
for without charity, let men have what gifts you please,
they are nothing.[26]
—Jonathan Edwards

I love being in the garden. I love it every time we plant a new plant or
when new sprouts come up in the spring. The beauty and fragrance
of the roses, black-eyed Susans, and echinacea make every visitor to
the garden smile. Birds fill the garden with their lovely songs and help

---

[25] A. W. Tozer, *The Pursuit of God: The Human Thirst for the Divine* (Project Gutenberg e-Book, 2008, first published in 1948), 22, Public domain in the USA.

[26] Jonathan Edwards, *Charity and Its Fruits: Or, Christian Love as Manifested in the Heart and Life* (United Kingdom: Robert Carter & Brothers, 1852).

to make the garden a place of peace. Gardening is work, but its benefits are amazing. The garden in many ways expresses love to all those that experience it, through gifts of produce and the blessing of peace.

God is love. All of the fruits of the Spirit are rooted in love. Without love, none of them can be achieved. As Jonathan Edwards stated in the quote at the opening of this chapter, "For without charity, let men have what gifts you please, they are nothing."[27] God is the Master Gardener, and in His garden, we can find perfect love and peace, so it makes sense that the greatest commandments in the Bible involve loving God and loving our neighbors.

> One of the scribes came and heard them arguing and, recognizing that He had answered them well, asked Him, "What commandment is the foremost of all?" Jesus answered, "The foremost is, 'HEAR, O ISRAEL! THE LORD OUR GOD IS ONE LORD; AND YOU SHALL LOVE THE LORD YOUR GOD WITH ALL YOUR HEART, AND WITH ALL YOUR SOUL, AND WITH ALL YOUR MIND, AND WITH ALL YOUR STRENGTH.' The second is this, 'YOU SHALL LOVE YOUR NEIGHBOR AS YOURSELF.' There is no other commandment greater than these." The scribe said to Him, "Right, Teacher; You have truly stated that HE IS ONE, AND THERE IS NO ONE ELSE BESIDES HIM; AND TO LOVE HIM WITH ALL THE HEART AND WITH ALL THE UNDERSTANDING AND WITH ALL THE STRENGTH, AND TO LOVE ONE'S NEIGHBOR AS HIMSELF, is much more than all burnt offerings and sacrifices." When Jesus saw that he had answered intelligently, He said to him, "You are not far from the kingdom of God." After that, no one would venture to ask Him any more questions. (Mark 12:28–34)

---

[27] Jonathan Edwards, *Charity and Its Fruits: Or, Christian Love as Manifested in the Heart and Life* (United Kingdom: Robert Carter & Brothers, 1852).

This passage in Mark is often quoted to remind us of our calling to love. We are called to love God with all of our heart, soul, mind, and strength, and love our neighbors as well. I'd like to focus on the scribe's response at the end of the passage. He affirms Jesus's words to love God and to love other people, and then he adds that to love this way is "much more than all burnt offerings and sacrifices" (verse 33). Merely loving God and worshipping Him only on Sunday mornings is similar to the scribes and Pharisees going to the temple and offering their sacrifices. If that is all there is, it's empty. To love with all of our heart, soul, mind, and strength requires action, not platitude. Our love for God is felt in our heart, believed in our soul, and studied and searched for with our mind; and with our physical strength, we do whatever He asks of us. If we truly love God with all of our being, He will be on our mind constantly. When I first met my future husband, and fell in love, I didn't only think of him and talk to him one day a week for a few minutes. He was on my mind from the moment I got up until I went to bed, and even in my dreams! I couldn't wait to talk to him. When someone gets into your heart, it is a natural consequence to be engulfed by thoughts of them. Similarly, when I first fell in love with Jesus, He was on my mind all the time. I remember when I first heard Him call to me. I didn't hear an actual voice, but I did feel Him calling me to pray and spend time with Him. I was just a kid at Camp Yamhill, a Christian summer youth camp in Yamhill, Oregon. I would sneak out of the cabin at night, much to the chagrin of my counselors, and run out to the woods to pray and be alone with Him. I couldn't wait to spend time with Him. I remember when I made the decision to be baptized, again at camp. They couldn't do the baptism without my parents' consent, so I had to wait until they could contact them. I was so frustrated because I knew it wasn't my parents' decision, it was mine, and I knew they would approve. I wanted to do whatever God asked of me. I didn't see the point of waiting until tomorrow. Such young and innocent faith! I strive to get back to that simple and trusting love. This is the kind of love God wants to share with us. It's the kind of love He wants us to share with those around us. He loves us, so we ought to love one another.

The love of God is amazing. He loves us so very much; it is sometimes difficult to wrap our minds around it. To explain that love to someone who doesn't know Him can be a challenge. Often people who don't know God see Him as cruel and unapproachable, vengeful, and distant. But the truth is far from that. God is love; it is the defining characteristic of His personality. A. W. Tozer in his book *The Knowledge of the Holy* wrote,

> Yet if we would know God and for other's sake tell what we know we must try to speak of his love. All Christians have tried but none has ever done it very well. I can no more do justice to that awesome and wonder-filled theme than a child can grasp a star. Still by reaching toward the star the child may call attention to it and even indicate the direction one must look to see it. So as I stretch my heart toward the high shining love of God someone who has not before known about it may be encouraged to look up and have hope.[28]

Love for God spills over onto those around us. As we reach for Him, others are encouraged to do the same. Our love for God is closely linked to our love for others. We love because He first loved us. Love is action—it's not just a statement of fact; "I love my neighbor" is proven in our actions. If we love God, we spend time with Him, studying, praying, worshipping. If we love our neighbor, we show it by spending time with them, being generous with what we have, caring for their needs, laughing with them, crying with them, praying for and with them. Love without action really isn't love at all; it's just a word without meaning in the same way that faith without works is a dead faith (James 2:17, 26). But if we have been saved and the Spirit of God lives within us, then our works are evidence of that fact. In the same way, our actions done in love are evidence of our love. Love without action means nothing. This is why we are encouraged by Paul in 1 Thessalonians 5:19 to not put out

---

[28] A. W. Tozer, *The Knowledge of the Holy*, (Harper Collins, 2009).

the Spirit's fire, to not quench the Spirit. It is the Spirit Who will guide us to actions that show our love. If we ignore Him and dismiss His leading, our faith and our love dwindle and become ineffective and lifeless.

Often, we, as Christians, are seeking spiritual euphoria in worship—a love-filled experience of the pouring out of the Spirit; we ask Him to come and fill the building with His Presence so we can connect with Him in love and praise. And that is an amazing experience! There is no greater feeling! But sometimes we forget that the Spirit is within us always if we are believers, constantly seeking love and relationship. He is encouraging and leading us every day, but how often do we ignore Him? If the Spirit leads us to connect with someone who is hurting, do we allow ourselves to get sidetracked and not follow through? Often, the Lord will bring to mind a specific person, and I know that He wants me to pray for them right then in that moment. I don't know what that person is going through, but the Spirit knows. Even in this simple thing, God is working in our hearts through His Spirit. His love is working in us and through us. In Romans 12:1, Paul tells us, "Therefore I urge you, brethren, by the mercies of God, to present your bodies a living and holy sacrifice, acceptable to God, which is your spiritual service of worship." Worship is not limited to Sunday morning services; it is more than singing songs of praise and prayer. According to this verse, it is worship to be wholly submitted to God. We should obey the Spirit every day of our lives with the same gusto we long for in praise and worship to Him.

To be a follower of Christ is to be loving. We love God with our whole being, and we love those around us and care for them. God is love, and we are to be love to the world. It means that we live our lives with God's love at our core. We love Him, and we love His word and obey it. We exist in His love and spread that love to the people around us. Jonathan Edwards expressed it this way:

> But it is doubtless true, and evident from [the] Scriptures, that the essence of all true religion lies in holy love; and that in this divine affection, and an habitual disposition to it, and that light which

is the foundation of it, and those things which are the fruits of it, consists the whole of religion.[29]

Edwards is saying that the entirety of religion is love—love for God first and foremost as the foundation and then love for others as the fruit of our love for God. We are called to be people ruled by the love of God. All of our actions and even our thoughts should be motivated by this love. If we love God, we will keep His commandments; if we love the people around us, we will care for their needs and share the goodness of God with them. For if this love is allowed to rule in our hearts, we will automatically become fruitful for God and on fire for His kingdom. His Spirit is within us, a beautiful gift from the Father, to guide us in His perfect love. If we are not loving people, we are not God's people. We must allow His love to permeate our souls and spill out onto the lives of the people around us. Just as the garden satisfies and blesses all those who enter, so we love and bless those whom God puts in our path.

> Beloved, let us love one another, for love is from God; and everyone who loves is born of God and knows God. The one who does not love does not know God, for God is love. By this the love of God was manifested in us, that God has sent His only begotten Son into the world so that we might live through Him. In this is love, not that we loved God, but that He loved us and sent His Son to be the propitiation for our sins. Beloved, if God so loved us, we also ought to love one another. No one has seen God at any time; if we love one another, God abides in us, and His love is perfected in us. By this we know that we abide in Him and He in us, because He has given us of His Spirit. We have seen and testify that the Father has sent the Son to be the Savior of the world. (1 John 4:7–14)

---

[29] Jonathan Edwards, *A Treatise Concerning Religious Affections* (Dublin: J. Ogle, 1812).

Questions to Consider

Chapter 6: Love

1. What is the greatest commandment in Scripture?

_____

_____

_____

_____

_____

_____

2. What is the second greatest commandment?

_____

_____

_____

_____

_____

3. What correlation is there between love for God and obedience to His word?

_____

_____

_____

_____

_____

4. In what ways can our love for God overflow onto the people around us?

_____

_____

_____

_____

Using the lines below, write out Colossians 3:14. Reread it many times during the week. Try to commit it to memory.

_____

_____

_____

_____

_____

_____

_____

_____

_____

_____

_____

_____

_____

_____

_____

_____

_____

_____

_____

_____

_____

_____

Holy God,

Thank You for Your amazing and everlasting love. Help us to love You more and more every day and to pour that love over those You put in our path.
In Jesus's name, amen.

CHAPTER 7

Joy

But let all who take refuge in You be glad, let them ever sing for joy;
and may You shelter them, that those who love Your name
may exult in You.

—Psalm 5:11

I grow plants for many reasons: to please my eye or
to please my soul, to challenge the elements or to
challenge my patience, for novelty or for nostalgia,
but mostly for the joy in seeing them grow.[30]

—David Hobson

Being in the garden on a warm summer day—the gentle breeze tickling the wind chimes; flowers blooming, their fragrance filling the air; birds and bees adding their voices to the symphony—brings an abundance of joy to my heart. A garden is a beautiful place, a place of peace and happiness. Planting and nurturing create in me a purpose: to achieve the beauty and joy of the thriving garden. The same is true for God's garden. Our goal is the beauty and joy of the kingdom of God.

What exactly is joy? *Merriam-Webster* defines *joy* as "the emotion evoked by well-being, success, or good fortune or by the prospect of possessing what one desires."[31] According to that definition, joy comes when everything is going great; we are having success and

---

[30] *The Ultimate Book of Quotations*, 155, Lulu.com.
[31] *Merriam-Webster Dictionary*, s.v. "Joy," accessed February 23, 2021, https://www.merriam-webster.com/dictionary/joy.

getting what we want. It would be assumed, then, that joy would disappear once our circumstances took a turn for the worse. This is the world's definition of joy, but the Christian definition runs deeper than our circumstance. We can have joy even in the midst of great struggle, loss, or pain. Nehemiah, the ruler of Judah during the exile to Babylon, gathered all the remnants of the Jews who had been left behind at the time of the exile; and he read to them the Law of Moses. This was to celebrate the rebuilding of the wall surrounding Jerusalem and also the Feast of Trumpets, which was their new year celebration. But instead of it being a time of happiness and joy, the people were weeping, convicted of their sin, because of the reading of the Law. Over the years, the Law had been neglected and forgotten. They realized that they had not been faithful to God and had not been obedient to His Law. But Nehemiah tells them to celebrate and not to grieve, for "the joy of the Lord is your strength" (Nehemiah 8:1–12). He encourages them and tells them that now they have the Law and can return to the Lord and be faithful again. They could have joy in the Lord, and He would strengthen them and sustain them. So even in the midst of sorrow and grief, joy is there. Joy in the Lord builds us up and gives us strength.

One of my favorite authors and preachers is John Piper. Mr. Piper is a theologian, an author, a pastor, the founder of DesiringGod.org, and the chancellor of Bethlehem College and Seminary in Minneapolis, Minnesota. He presented a sermon entitled "How Do You Define Joy?" In this sermon, he gave his definition of Christian *joy*.

> Christian joy is a good feeling in the soul, pro-
> duced by the Holy Spirit, as He causes us to
> see the beauty of Christ in the word and in the
> world.[32]

Mr. Piper said that joy is a feeling produced by the Holy Spirit, and this is a key difference between worldly joy and heavenly joy. We, as Christians, can feel peace and acceptance even in the middle

---

[32] John Piper, "How Do You Define Joy?" DesiringGod.org, July 25, 2015.

of a crisis because the Holy Spirit is within us. Remember, the fruits of the Spirit do not come about by our own design or effort—they are gifts from the Spirit of God. We have godly joy because we have the Spirit of Christ indwelling us. It is not always a deliriously happy kind of joy—laughing in the face of adversity—but a sense of contentment, knowing that nothing can separate us from His love. In Paul's letter to the Thessalonians, he commends them for their earnest seeking after God, even through affliction and trouble.

> We give thanks to God always for all of you, making mention of you in our prayers; constantly bearing in mind your work of faith and labor of love and steadfastness of hope in our Lord Jesus Christ in the presence of our God and Father, knowing, brethren beloved by God, His choice of you; for our gospel did not come to you in word only, but also in power and in the Holy Spirit and with full conviction; just as you know what kind of men we proved to be among you for your sake. You also became imitators of us and of the Lord, having received the word in much tribulation with the joy of the Holy Spirit, so that you became an example to all the believers. (1 Thessalonians 1:2–7)

Paul here states that they received the word with the joy of the Holy Spirit. We can draw a couple of interesting thoughts from this phrase. First, we experience joy when we interact with the Spirit of God. His Presence in our lives makes us different from the world because we have the Creator dwelling within us. The hopelessness and despair of this world no longer control us, even when times are difficult, because we have at our core eternal peace and joy, knowing that the Spirit is with us, that God is in control and that our eternity is secure. It doesn't mean we will never feel anxious, overwhelmed, or depressed; but in the midst of all that, we have a confidence—a firm foundation—that speaks peace and assurance to our soul. This is the Spirit of God, and He brings a deep and abiding joy.

The second truth found in Paul's passage in 1 Thessalonians is that receiving the word brings joy—not merely reading or quoting it but receiving it. Remember the parable of the sower and the different types of soil? Receiving the word means planting it deep into your heart, not just on the surface where it can be quickly forgotten or snatched away. Dig deep into Scripture; study it; pray over it, asking God to guide your understanding; share it; and most importantly, apply it to your life. This act produces joy in the Holy Spirit. Think about a time when you were studying the word and a certain passage spoke to you—clearly convicting you or touching your heart in a way that could only be from the Spirit, perhaps immediately bringing you to tears or sending chills down the back of your neck. Our joy is full when we interact with the Spirit of God and receive His word into our hearts. This is the joy of the Holy Spirit! The joy of the Lord gives us strength through His Spirit within us, but our discussion of joy isn't complete without remembering the joy of our salvation. In Peter's first letter, he reminds us of this great gift of salvation.

> Blessed be the God and Father of our Lord Jesus Christ, who according to His great mercy has caused us to be born again to a living hope through the resurrection of Jesus Christ from the dead, to obtain an inheritance which is imperishable and undefiled and will not fade away, reserved in heaven for you, who are protected by the power of God through faith for a salvation ready to be revealed in the last time. In this you greatly rejoice, even though now for a little while, if necessary, you have been distressed by various trials, so that the proof of your faith, being more precious than gold which is perishable, even though tested by fire, may be found to result in praise and glory and honor at the revelation of Jesus Christ; and though you have not seen Him,

you love Him, and though you do not see Him now, but believe in Him, you greatly rejoice with joy inexpressible and full of glory, obtaining as the outcome of your faith the salvation of your souls. (1 Peter 1:3–9)

What a beautiful description of what God is for us in Christ Jesus! Salvation—this amazing gift of God—produces joy inexpressible and full of glory! Let us never allow ourselves to become passive about this or to forget what glory awaits us and what glory exists within us right now. We are saved, *not* by anything we've done but by God's grace and mercy. When I committed my life to God and was baptized, I was filled with such joy, an overwhelming sense of His *presence*. Even now, decades later, when I think about that day—the confession that I made and the song that was sung as I came out of the water—I still get goose bumps, and tears well up in my eyes. Remember always the joy of your salvation! Jonathan Edwards, in one of his writings entitled "A Treatise Concerning Religious Affections," wrote this about the joy expressed in 1 Peter 1:8:

Their joy was full of glory. Although the joy was unspeakable, and no words were sufficient to describe it; yet something might be said of it, and no words more fit to represent its excellency than these, that it was full of glory; or, as it is in the original, glorified joy. In rejoicing with this joy, their minds were filled, as it were, with a glorious brightness, and their natures exalted and perfected. It was a most worthy, noble rejoicing, that did not corrupt and debase the mind, as many carnal joys do; but did greatly beautify and dignify it. It was a prelibation of the joy of heaven, that raised their minds to a degree of heavenly blessedness; it filled their minds with the light of

God's glory, and made themselves to shine with
some communication of that glory.[33]

Joy unspeakable! Joy so amazing there are no words to describe
its beauty. Joy that is a taste of the divine, a touch of heaven. This is
true joy, and it is contagious and attractive! One of the most mem-
orable Bible verses on this topic is found in Psalm 51. David wrote
this psalm after his sin with Bathsheba, and he is pleading for God's
forgiveness and restoration of their relationship.

> Be gracious to me, O God, according to Your
> lovingkindness;
> According to the greatness of Your compassion
> blot out my transgressions.
> Wash me thoroughly from my iniquity
> And cleanse me from my sin.
> For I know my transgressions,
> And my sin is ever before me.
> Against You, You only, I have sinned
> And done what is evil in Your sight,
> So that You are justified when You speak
> And blameless when You judge.
> Behold, I was brought forth in iniquity,
> And in sin my mother conceived me.
> Behold, You desire truth in the innermost being,
> And in the hidden part You will make me know
> wisdom.
> Purify me with hyssop, and I shall be clean;
> Wash me, and I shall be whiter than snow.
> Make me to hear joy and gladness,
> Let the bones which You have broken rejoice.
> Hide Your face from my sins

---

[33] Jonathan Edwards, "A Treatise Concerning Religious Affections," *The Complete Works of Jonathan Edwards: Christ Exalted, Sinners in the Hands of the Angry God, a Divine and Supernatural Light, Christian Knowledge*...(fifty-nine books with active table of contents), 534–535, Kindle Edition.

And blot out all my iniquities.
Create in me a clean heart, O God,
And renew a steadfast spirit within me.
Do not cast me away from Your presence
And do not take Your Holy Spirit from me.
Restore to me the joy of Your salvation
And sustain me with a willing spirit.
Then I will teach transgressors Your ways,
And sinners will be converted to You.
(Psalm 51:1–13)

The last few verses of this psalm are so beautiful, a heartfelt plea for forgiveness and purification, an earnest desire for renewal. Don't cast me away or take your Spirit from me. Restore the joy that has been lost because of my sin. David is pleading with God to restore the joy of his salvation, to put himself in right standing with God again. How many times have we prayed the same prayer? But we often leave off the last verse of this passage, which is so very important. "Then I will teach transgressors your ways, and sinners will be converted to you." Restore my joy and make me steadfast; then I can teach others. Joy is attractive. People are drawn to it—whether it is an outward, genuine happiness that sparkles in the eyes, or the deep, abiding confidence that, even in trials, speaks of a strong faith in God. People want to experience this kind of joy—the world has nothing to compare with it. The best the world can offer is materialism or fleshly indulgence or possibly the happiness of family, although that is fading away as well, with the deterioration of the family unit. Only in Christ is true joy found. Not only is this joy attractive to others, but joy also brings out in us a higher calling—a desire to serve those around us. Worldly joy is often self-centered; what makes me happy gives me joy. It is often materialistic—more toys, bigger houses, fancier cars, nicer clothes, more, more, more; or often, it is self-indulgent which expresses itself in abuses with alcohol, drugs, food, or even too much work or exercise. While these things may bring joy in the moment, the end result is usually destructive and self-serving. Making ourselves happy does nothing for the people around us.

Christian joy, on the other hand, is God-centered; what makes Him happy gives me joy. It brings great joy when we meet the needs of the people around us. We feel joy when we provide food for the hungry or clothes for those in need. When we help someone who is struggling, we experience joy. If we are able to financially assist a family in need, we feel God's joy. When we share His love and the good news of salvation with a hungry soul, God's joy fills our soul, and our joy is full because of the debt that Jesus paid on our behalf. It is such a great joy to bring someone to the Lord! Through this joy, we become more fruitful for God. Just as the garden makes joyful those who experience its beauty, so we as God's garden bring joy to the people around us, through His love and His Spirit within us. It is God's joy that emanates through us and returns back to Him. To quote again from Jonathan Edwards,

> The beams of glory come from God, are something of God, and are refunded back again to their original. So that the whole is of God, and in God, and to God; and he is the beginning, and the middle, and the end.[34]

---

[34] Jonathan Edwards, "Dissertation of the End for Which God Created the World," *The Complete Works of Jonathan Edwards*, 84, Kindle Edition.

Questions to Consider

Chapter 7: Joy

1. How does the joy of the Lord differ from the world's definition?

_____

_____

_____

_____

_____

2. How does receiving the word of God give us joy?

_____

_____

_____

_____

_____

3. In what ways is true joy absent in today's world apart from God?

_____

_____

_____

_____

_____

4. In what ways does the joy of the Lord help us bear fruit?

_____

_____

_____

_____

_____

Using the lines below, write out Psalm 5:11. Reread it many times during the week. Try to commit it to memory.

_____
_____
_____
_____
_____
_____
_____
_____
_____
_____
_____
_____
_____
_____
_____
_____
_____
_____
_____
_____
_____
_____
_____
_____

Father God,

In Your joy, we find great strength. Thank You for the joy of Your Spirit within us. Remind us always of the joy of Your salvation. In Jesus's name, amen.

CHAPTER 8

Peace

Let the peace of Christ rule in your hearts, to which
indeed you were called in one body; and be thankful.
—Colossians 3:15

Peace I leave with you; My peace I give to you;
not as the world gives do I give to you. Do not let
your heart be troubled, nor let it be fearful.
—John 14:27

When the worries and stresses of this life start to weigh me down,
often I will go to the garden. In the sweet days of summer, the garden helps me to breathe. The fragrant flowers and earthy smell of
freshly turned soil, the singing of the birds and the buzzing of the
bees, the gentle wind ringing the chimes and rustling through the
leaves—I shut my eyes and soak in the peace. Even in the winter
months, when the garden is sleeping and the winter weather prevents
me from dwelling there, I will go to the window overlooking the garden and breathe. I watch the birds at the feeders and the free-ranging
chickens, and I soak in the view and still feel the peace. A garden is
a peaceful place.

Peace, the third attribute of the fruits of the Spirit, is most often
thought of as an absence of conflict, a time when fighting ceases.
When defined on a personal level, it refers to a feeling of serenity
or tranquility within a person's soul, regardless of outward circumstances. In this way, it is very closely associated with joy, a knowledge
that God is in control regardless of the chaos surrounding us.

As I am writing this, we are in the middle of the chaos of the 2020 election. COVID-19 is still running rampant. Lockdowns are still in effect. Rioting and protesting are a daily occurrence in the cities. There are divisions and hatred everywhere. Tensions are running high… It is anything but peaceful. Some days, I wish I could just run away and escape to a high mountain lake or stream and just "be." To get away from the stress and angst of society and dangle my toes in the cool water while I wait for a fish to take my hook. There are far too few "quiet waters" these days. But stress and anxiety are nothing new. People have been struggling with this since the very beginning. How many times did Jesus go off by Himself to pray and get away from the crowds? In Mark 6, it is recorded that Jesus and His apostles were gathered together after the apostles' return from a preaching tour. When returning home from a trip, most people are ready to crash for a while—to regain their strength after being away. It was no different for the apostles.

> The apostles gathered together with Jesus, and they reported to Him all that they had done and taught. And He said to them, "Come away by yourselves to a secluded place and rest a while." (For there were many people coming and going, and they did not even have time to eat.) They went away in the boat to a secluded place by themselves.
>
> The people saw them going, and many recognized them and ran there together on foot from all the cities, and got there ahead of them. When Jesus went ashore, He saw a large crowd, and He felt compassion for them because they were like sheep without a shepherd; and He began to teach them many things. When it was already quite late, His disciples came to Him and said, "This place is desolate and it is already quite late; send them away so that they may go into the surrounding countryside and villages and buy themselves

something to eat." But He answered them, "You give them something to eat!" And they said to Him, "Shall we go and spend two hundred denarii on bread and give them something to eat?" And He said to them, "How many loaves do you have? Go look!" And when they found out, they said, "Five, and two fish." And He commanded them all to sit down by groups on the green grass. They sat down in groups of hundreds and of fifties. And He took the five loaves and the two fish, and looking up toward heaven, He blessed the food and broke the loaves and He kept giving them to the disciples to set before them; and He divided up the two fish among them all. They all ate and were satisfied, and they picked up twelve full baskets of the broken pieces, and also of the fish. There were five thousand men who ate the loaves.

Immediately Jesus made His disciples get into the boat and go ahead of Him to the other side to Bethsaida, while He Himself was sending the crowd away. After bidding them farewell, He left for the mountain to pray. (Mark 6:30–46)

There were so many people around that they hadn't had time to rest or even eat. I can imagine the apostles were tired and hungry and anxious to tell Jesus everything they had experienced while they were away. Jesus's response to them was, "Come away by yourselves to a secluded place and rest a while" (Mark 6:31). What a beautiful thought! So they sailed off across the Sea of Galilee. They were no doubt exhausted physically, mentally, and spiritually. The rocking of the boat on the water and the chance to rest with Jesus—what a peaceful image that brings to my mind. For me, it seems peaceful scenes often tend to involve water. The gentle sound of water lapping at the sides of the boat and the up-and-down motion of the boat lulls into complete relaxation. Jesus knew that they needed that kind of downtime. After all, they could have walked just as the crowds of people did, but the boat offered a few minutes of rest and solitude. However, it was short-lived, as the crowds saw them go and ran ahead and got there before them. Jesus, though, in His great love and compassion didn't get upset but gave them all a meal instead. After that, He sent the disciples back across the Sea, dismissed the crowds, and went off by Himself to pray. He, too, needed a break from the crowds. And this is the peace He gives us: to face every obstacle, every frustration, with the confidence that God will get us through it. But it is not merely a suggestion in Scripture. In Colossians 3:15, Paul writes, "Let the peace of Christ rule in your hearts, to which indeed you were called in one body." Peace should rule! It should not take a backseat to our circumstances or our feelings in any given moment. Peace should be our goal or aim in every situation. It should take priority. We should not allow our circumstances to dictate our hearts. Our hearts, our souls, belong to the Almighty God, purchased with the blood of Jesus Christ. His Spirit lives within us; therefore, we are called to peace. As the body of Christ, we are encouraged to live in peace, seeking and pursuing it with the help and guidance of the Holy Spirit. The Spirit blesses us with His gift of peace.

In Romans 12:18, Paul states, "As far as it depends on you, be at peace with all men." Even if everyone around us is in conflict, we should be at peace. This doesn't mean that we will always be happy in every situation, but we are at peace, knowing that God is Sovereign and in control. It also doesn't mean we have to "cave" on our beliefs or silence our opinions in order to have peace, but peace is to rule. Nowhere does God tell us that our opinions must be heard or that opinions should rule or guide us. Can you imagine the chaos that would cause? Well, maybe you can. Just turn on the news or spend a few minutes on social media, and you will see plenty of it. But the Spirit of God leads us in a different direction. God tells us that His peace will protect our hearts and our minds, so even in disagreements, the peace of God controls us.

Be anxious for nothing, but in everything by prayer and supplication with thanksgiving let your requests be made known to God. And the peace of God, which surpasses all comprehension, will guard your hearts and your minds in Christ Jesus.

Finally, brethren, whatever is true, whatever is honorable, whatever is right, whatever is pure, whatever is lovely, whatever is of good repute, if there is any excellence and if anything worthy of praise, dwell on these things. The things you have learned and received and heard and seen in me, practice these things, and the God of peace will be with you. (Philippians 4:7–9)

Having a peaceful nature breaks down conflict. It is difficult for someone to have an argument with you if you refuse to argue. It takes the wind out of their sails. There will always be those around us who seem to live for the argument, and social media is the worst for this kind of behavior. I have had folks on social media who are basically invisible friends... They never like or comment on anything until I post something they have a differing opinion about, and then it's full-on attack mode, forcing their opinions on me with harsh words and a serious lack of peace. These people haven't had any concern for my life up to that point but feel they have the right to "put me in my place" on social media. This is not good. We are called to peace, not chaos, not arguments. Paul tells us to "follow after the things that make for peace" (Romans 14:19). Sometimes, that means disengaging from those who only want to fight and argue. Taking occasional breaks from social media can do wonders for your overall peace.

The peace of Christ is all-encompassing. It changes how we view our daily circumstances. How could Paul and Silas praise God while in chains in a prison cell? How could Stephen give praise to the Lord as he was being stoned to death? How could Jesus, on the Cross, in extreme pain and intense suffering say, "Forgive them"? It is because they took their thoughts captive and allowed the peace of God to dominate their minds. This is an area that I struggle with: when someone verbally attacks me and treats me badly, I go into full-on self-protection mode, hackles raised, and fangs bared. My first instinct is definitely not to be at peace—to forgive or sing songs of praise. I've got a long way to go. It is the Spirit Who gives us this kind of peace, and it takes practice to fully develop. I must learn to stop in the moment when I am being defensive and allow God to be my Sword and Shield. It is the peace of Christ that enables us to endure in whatever circumstance we find ourselves. This peace has no comparison in the world. The closest relation is to be free from strife or conflict; but to have peace in the middle of strife or conflict, that is divine, born of the Spirit. Jerry Bridges (1929–2016), an evangelical Christian author and speaker, wrote many books, including *The Practice of Godliness*. In this book, he explains how peace should be a characteristic of all followers of Christ.

> Peace should be a hallmark of the godly person, first because it is a Godlike trait: God is called the God of peace several times in the New Testament. He took the initiative to establish peace with rebellious men, and He is the author of both personal peace as well as peace among men. Peace should be part of our character also because God has promised us His peace, because He has commanded us to let peace rule in our lives and relationships, and because peace is a fruit of the Spirit and, therefore, an evidence of His working in our lives.[35]

Peace, divine peace, is proof that the Spirit of God is active in our lives. People in today's world long for this peace that passes understanding, that fills the soul with confidence that Someone is in control. They may not know Him, but they long for Him all the same. Jesus Christ offers this peace to a broken and chaotic world which desperately needs Him. In God's garden, there is peace—a place where we can stop all the stressing and just breathe in the beau-

---

[35] Jerry Bridges, *The Practice of Godliness* (Colorado Springs: Navpress, 1983), 155–156.

tiful and soothing fragrance of His Presence. He says, "These things I have spoken to you, so that in Me you may have peace. In the world you have tribulation, but take courage; I have overcome the world" (John 16:33).

"Peace in Jesus"
By Archibald Kenyon

Oh the peace that in Jesus I find!
How it cheers me amid all my care;
It is sweet to the sorrowing mind,
In this precious salvation to share.
Yes, I know that my Saviour is mine,
That He never will leave me to die;
Tho' in weakness I often repine,
He will fill all my soul by and by.
By His Spirit He dwells with me now,
And His voice is so gentle and still;
As before Him in worship I bow,
It is sweet to submit to His will.
then still nearer to Him may I live;
More and more of His love, is my prayer;
Every blessing I need will He give,
And receive me at home over there.
O the peace, sweet peace
That my Saviour has given to me![36]

---

[36] Archibald Kenyon, arr. by Robert Lowry, "Peace in Jesus," Public Domain in the USA.

Questions to Consider

Chapter 8: Peace

1. What are some ways you can find God's peace in the midst of strife?

   _____

   _____

   _____

   _____

   _____

2. How does God's peace break down conflict?

   _____

   _____

   _____

   _____

   _____

3. How does God's peace guard your heart and mind?

   _____

   _____

   _____

   _____

   _____

4. Think of a scripture or song that brings to your mind the peace of God. Write it out below.

   _____

   _____

   _____

   _____

   _____

Using the lines below, write out John 14:27. Reread it many times during the week. Try to commit it to memory.

_____
_____
_____
_____
_____
_____
_____
_____
_____
_____
_____
_____
_____
_____
_____
_____
_____
_____
_____
_____
_____
_____
_____
_____
_____
_____
_____
_____

Our Father in heaven,

Thank You for Your peace that passes understanding. Guide us to be peace-loving people. In Jesus's name, amen.

CHAPTER 9

Patience

A garden is a grand teacher. It teaches patience and
careful watchfulness; it teaches industry and thrift;
above all it teaches entire trust.[37]

—Gertrude Jekyll

Genius is eternal patience.

—Michelangelo

Those who wait for the LORD will gain new strength; they will
mount up with wings like eagles, they will run and not get tired,
they will walk and not become weary.

—Isaiah 40:31

I remember, when I was little, planting green bean seeds in a paper cup.
I watered them and put the cup on the windowsill where it would get
the most sunlight, and I waited...not patiently. The next day, I stuck
my fingers into the dirt and dug out the seeds to see if they were growing
yet. I remember my mom and dad trying to explain to me that it would
take time for the seeds to grow, and I needed to be patient. Gardening
requires patience. We put a lot of work into preparing the soil, weeding,
and caring for the plants; and then we wait for the harvest. Sometimes,
we see fruit within a few weeks, and sometimes, it takes months or even
years, but still we wait with hopeful expectation for the fruits of our
labor. Waiting is hard... Waiting patiently is even harder.

---

[37] Gertrude Jekyll, *Gertrude Jekyll on Gardening* (Vintage Books, 1985), 26.

Patience is defined as "the capacity to accept or tolerate delay, trouble, or suffering without getting angry or upset."[38] It is often synonymous with endurance or perseverance. How many of us struggle with this issue? Does our society tolerate a delay when we want something right now...without getting angry or upset? Ummm... not so much. Spend some time in traffic or in a long, slow-moving line at the DMV, and you may see evidence of this. If sickness, crisis, or even petty inconvenience touches our life or the life of a loved one, do we accept it without anger or upset, or do we blame God or other people for causing us pain and trouble?

When I was a young woman, my patience was seriously tested, as I anxiously waited to meet that special someone I would eventually marry. I had such high hopes. As the years passed, friend after friend married, set up their homes, and became parents and even grandparents, while still I waited. How many prayers did I pray for God to help me find my perfect mate? I can't say that I was successful with my test of patience; there were definitely days and weeks and months and years when I struggled with it. Dating was unsuccessful and discouraging. Men I thought were "perfect" for me turned out to be disappointing, to say the least. People would make comments about my singleness that were not always kind. Judgments were made about my "life choice." (When did I "choose" to be single? I don't remember checking that box!) I felt isolated at church, because church is a family-centered body, and a single doesn't always feel like they fit in. Friends moved away to start their lives or were busy raising their families. But over the years, I endured, never giving up my prayer; and finally, at age fifty, I decided to try the new craze of online dating. It was my Year of Jubilee,[39] and God blessed me abundantly with the most wonderful man I could ever have hoped for. I know during the long, lonely years, God was my Refuge and my Strength.

---

[38] *Google's English Dictionary—Oxford Languages*, s.v. "Patience" (Oxford University Press, 2020).

[39] In Israel, every fifty years was the Year of Jubilee, when debts were erased, slaves were released, and property reverted back to its original owner. This was a year of rest dedicated to God and an acknowledgment that He has provided for their needs.

True patience, deep, abiding patience does not come from our own effort... It is not a natural response to struggles. It is divine, born of the Spirit of God. To endure or persevere through tough times requires a reliance on God—a knowledge that He is above all and will carry us through, to fill our minds with His word and trust Him. In Romans 15, Paul writes,

> For whatever was written in earlier times was written for our instruction, so that through perseverance and the encouragement of the Scriptures we might have hope. Now may the God who gives perseverance and encouragement grant you to be of the same mind with one another according to Christ Jesus, so that with one accord you may with one voice glorify the God and Father of our Lord Jesus Christ. (Romans 15:4–6)

Notice how Paul points out that the Scriptures provide perseverance and encouragement and that these attributes are from God. So how can we hope to persevere or patiently endure without Him? The Spirit of God within believers enables us to do what is impossible without Him. His word gives us the encouragement to keep going and to wait patiently for what He has prepared for us. The word of God is powerful; we should spend more time consuming it. In the Scriptures, we find hope and strength. God speaks to us through His word, giving us fortitude and determination, knowing He is in control.

God never promised us an easy life, free from struggle or trouble. On the contrary, He promises that "when" we go through struggles, He will be with us. "Even though I walk through the valley of the shadow of death, I fear no evil, for you are with me" (Psalm 23:4). Trials and troubles will come on us all, but we must lean on God and wait patiently for Him. The Bible is filled with verses that speak to this idea. Here are just a few:

> Consider it all joy, my brethren, when you encounter various trials, knowing that the testing of your

faith produces endurance. And let endurance have its perfect result, so that you may be perfect and complete, lacking in nothing. (James 1:2–4)

Blessed is a man who perseveres under trial; for once he has been approved, he will receive the crown of life which the Lord has promised to those who love Him. (James 1:12)

But resist him (the devil), firm in your faith, knowing that the same experiences of suffering are being accomplished by your brethren who are in the world. After you have suffered for a little while, the God of all grace, who called you to His eternal glory in Christ, will Himself perfect, confirm, strengthen and establish you. (1 Peter 5:9–10)

For I consider that the sufferings of this present time are not worthy to be compared with the glory that is to be revealed to us. (Romans 8:18)

All of these scriptures encourage us to be patient, to accept whatever is happening at the moment without anger or upset, to even have joy in the midst of it, knowing that God is with us and a glorious day is coming! We need to keep a heavenly perspective, to look beyond the immediate to the eternal. If we see the people around us through that lens, it will change how we interact with them. If the clerk at the grocery store is struggling with the computer, do I get upset that she is holding me up, or do I use the opportunity to share God's love and mercy with her? If I'm stuck in traffic, do I vent and fume over it, or do I take the time to talk with God or turn on some God music and sing praises? It is a matter of perspective. Turn our eyes on Jesus. "Run with endurance the race that is set before us, fixing our eyes on Jesus, the author and perfecter of faith" (Hebrews 12:1–2). If we view our struggles and trials through the lens of faith, we will gain strength to endure and rise above our difficulties. This strength is not from ourselves but from God, through His Spirit within us. "Those who wait for the LORD will gain new strength; they will mount up with wings like eagles, they will run and not get tired, they will walk and not become weary" (Isaiah 40:31).

Patience is a Spirit-driven characteristic. We are not patient by nature, quite the opposite. We are patient when we allow the Spirit of God within us to have sway over our natural tendency to stomp our feet and demand what we want, immediately when we want it. His Spirit reins in our impatient anger and desire for retaliation when we are wronged or mistreated. With His strength, we can breathe and maintain our cool, even when everything seems to fall apart. This is a reflection of His patience toward us. His patience with us is incredible. Isn't that a wonderful thing, for where would we be without His long-suffering patience with us? John MacArthur, in a sermon on the fruit of the Spirit, speaks about how patience is a work of the Spirit in our lives.

> In Colossians 1, "Walk in a manner worthy"—very much like Ephesians 4—"bearing fruit in every good work, increasing in the knowledge of God; strengthened with all power"—by the Holy Spirit, of course—"according to His glorious might, for the attaining of all steadfastness and patience." I don't know if you think of patience as a primary work of the Spirit of God in your life, but it is. If you don't have patience with those who offend you and those who disrupt your direction, those who invade your life, create havoc and chaos for you, if you don't have patience with them, you are not Christlike, and you are not manifesting the fruit of the Spirit. Your lives should be patience personified.
>
> Where does this come from? Well, obviously it comes from the Holy Spirit. And we just read Colossians 1. Paul says, "Since the day we heard of it, we have not ceased to pray for you and ask that you may be filled with"—and go down the list—"all patience; giving thanks to the Father."

> God is the source of this patience. Christ is the
> example of this patience. The Holy Spirit is the
> dispenser of this patience.[40]

If we are constantly struggling with impatience, we are not demonstrating Christlike behavior. We need to put aside our carnal, fleshly nature and allow the Spirit to lead us, to rein in our anger and selfishness and allow Him to guide us and control our situations. This is not always going to be easy, but God promises that He won't give us any trial that we cannot handle.

Early in my teaching career, education in our state took several financial hits, and my little district was suffering a critical financial shortfall. Being a relatively new hire, I was one of several teachers who were laid off. I was devastated and heartbroken. I prayed earnestly for a job. How could this happen to me? For a while, I was not patient. I felt desperate, but after a *lot* of prayer and running to the Father, I arrived at a place of peace, knowing God would take care of me. That was probably a tough year for me financially, but I don't remember those details. What I do remember is substitute teaching, getting to see how all these other teachers set up their rooms, how they handled classroom discipline, and the like—ideas that later greatly benefitted my own classroom. During this time of waiting, I was also asked by the parents of my district to prepare and direct the kids Christmas program, as the music teacher had also been laid off. I wound up having such a great time with the kids I forgot how miserable I was for losing my job. After a year of this, the district recalled me to my previous position. This year of waiting turned out to be one of the best in my memory and benefitted my career in many ways in the long run. Even in difficult times, when we feel there is no good end, God is still working. He will carry us through; we need to trust Him and remain faithful as we wait for Him.

Patience and endurance have a direct relationship with bearing fruit for God. It is difficult to see the needs of others when we are

---

[40] John MacArthur, "The Fruit of the Spirit, part 3," Grace to You, gty.org, © 2021, Used by permission.

consumed with our own needs. When we are impatient with people or impatient with God's timing, we make ourselves unfruitful. We get lost in ourselves. Bearing fruit becomes difficult because we can't take our eyes off ourselves long enough to see the others around us. However, when we are patient, we allow God to deal with our issues and problems; we take our eyes off ourselves and can focus on the people around us.

Patience also means being willing to wait for what God has in store. When we share God's love with people, we may not immediately see the results. It may take a long time. In fact, we may never see the results. But we keep on doing what the Spirit leads us to do. We bear fruit when we share God's word with others, when we give generously, when we pray for those in need, and when we continue on with these actions even if we don't see immediate results. There have been people in my life with whom I have shared the gospel, who chose to walk away from Christ. That can be so discouraging. But the seed had been planted, and who knows who might come into their lives at a later date and cultivate that seed? Sometimes, it takes years for a seed to sprout. With patience, we continue to water it and give it sunshine and nutrients. God provides the growth; our job is to continue doing what He calls us to do, without getting caught up in impatience or wanting to give up. We endure and patiently wait for the Lord. Just like the seeds in the paper cup, if cared for, will sprout and grow; so it is with the seeds we plant in the hearts of the people around us. One person plants and another waters, but God gives the increase.

Questions to Consider

Chapter 9: Patience

1. Under what circumstances do you find that your patience is the shortest?

_____

_____

_____

_____

_____

2. Tell about a time in your life when you needed enduring patience?

_____

_____

_____

_____

_____

3. Give an example of how the word of God helps us to have patience.

_____

_____

_____

_____

_____

4. How can patience help us bear fruit for God?

_____

_____

_____

_____

_____

Using the lines below, write out Isaiah 40:31. Reread it many times during the week. Try to commit it to memory.

_____

_____

_____

_____

_____

_____

_____

_____

_____

_____

_____

_____

_____

_____

_____

_____

_____

_____

_____

_____

_____

_____

_____

_____

_____

_____

_____

_____

Father God,

Thank You for being our Rock and our Fortress. Help us to endure the struggles in our lives with patience and perseverance through Your Spirit within us.
In Jesus's name, amen.

CHAPTER 10

Kindness and Goodness

Constant kindness can accomplish much.
As the sun makes ice melt, kindness causes misunderstanding,
mistrust, and hostility to evaporate.[41]

—Albert Schweitzer

I expect to pass through life but once. If therefore, there be
any kindness I can show, or any good thing I can do to any
fellow being, let me do it now, and not defer or neglect it,
as I shall not pass this way again.

—William Penn

Don't judge each day by the harvest you reap,
but by the seeds that you plant.[42]

—Robert Louis Stevenson

A garden exudes kindness and goodness. If a garden were a person,
you could easily describe her as kind and good. She gives her produce as well as her blossoms and serenity to all who enter in. Each
new day is greeted with blessings, from one end of the garden to
the other. The beautiful display of flowers in every color surrounds
the garden, inviting the bees and hummingbirds to visit, providing
a fragrant and lovely place for us to inhabit. Walking through the

---

[41] Jennifer Lee, *The Book of Quotes* (2020), 41.

[42] "Robert Louis Stevenson Quotes," BrainyQuote.com, BrainyMedia Inc., accessed 1 March 2021, http://www.brainyquote.com/quotes/robert_louis_stevenson_101230.

rows of berries, sampling the sweetness of the fruit on a summer day is a treat. Gathering the abundance of fruits and vegetables to share, to can, and to enjoy is such a gift. Gardens take work; they require commitment and perseverance; and after all that, they give back a bountiful harvest. Man's first habitation was in a setting such as this. Of all the habitats God could have created for Adam and Eve, He chose a garden, beautiful and abundant. When walking through our garden, I am reminded of God's infinite kindness and goodness and His great love for us.

Treating your garden with kindness and doing good works in your garden will produce good results. It is the same in our endeavors to bear fruit for God. We must treat the people around us with kindness and goodness. Being kind seems like such a simple concept. Everybody knows we should be kind. It's like a no-brainer—of course we should. And yet it seems to be something we, as a society, struggle with acting out. In fact, many times we show the least amount of kindness and goodness to the people we love the most—our family. The Spirit of God within us has planted the seeds of kindness and goodness, and we need to cultivate them.

To be kind, according to *Merriam-Webster*, means to be "of a sympathetic or helpful nature; forbearing; to give pleasure or relief."[43] It is synonymous with being attentive, considerate, thoughtful, courteous, gracious, merciful, or service oriented. Goodness is similar in its definition. Kindness, benevolence, loyalty, decency, honesty, righteousness, and virtuousness all are synonymous with goodness. At times, we might think that being kind is the same as being nice, which is defined as being courteous or proper. But it is so much more than a fake smile or a passing acknowledgment of someone. Kindness is action. To do good is an act of kindness.

Kindness can take many different forms. It can be an encouraging card, email, or phone call to someone you know is struggling; reaching out to the sick or shut-ins; giving generously to help those in poverty; donating items to help others; sending a meal to a family

---

[43] *Merriam-Webster Dictionary*, s.v. "Kindness," accessed February 23, 2021, https://www.merriam-webster.com/dictionary/kindness.

in need; cleaning the home of an elderly person or mowing their lawn; supporting single parents with free babysitting; becoming a support for a child in foster care. There are so many ways to be kind. These are only a few. But all of these actions have something in common: all of them are acts which benefit others, not acts which benefit the giver in any selfish or materialistic way. Is it true kindness when you do good for someone but have an ulterior motive? Perhaps it's pride—to be seen by others or to gain some standing or reputation as a kind and good person. These are self-serving motivations—and while good is still being done, God sees the intention of the heart. This type of kindness will inevitably be short-lived and lead to burn out because it is not from the heart. To be kind means we get out of our self-centered mind-set and see the needs of the people around us. We do not do it to be rewarded or to get a pat on the back. Spirit-led kindness and goodness come from the heart of God. So we do our best to be generous and to share what we have. It is good to share—our parents taught us that early on. Giving, sharing, generosity—these are characteristics of God's people and evidence of our faith. In Hebrews 13:6, Paul writes, "And do not neglect doing good and sharing, for with such sacrifices God is pleased." Sharing and being kind are sacrifices. It does require putting our own needs on the back burner. Selfishness or hoarding the blessings God has given us does not honor Him. Everything God blesses us with can be turned into an act of kindness.

The Spirit of God gives each of us gifts that we can use in serving Him and others around us. In 1 Peter 4, Peter states,

> As each one has received a special gift, employ it in serving one another as good stewards of the manifold grace of God. Whoever speaks, is to do so as one who is speaking the utterances of God; whoever serves is to do so as one who is serving by the strength which God supplies; so that in all things God may be glorified through Jesus Christ, to whom belongs the glory and dominion forever and ever. Amen. (1 Peter 4:10–11)

Has He blessed you with an abundance of money or material possessions or food? Give generously to others. Has He blessed you with an ability, for example, to bake or craft or teach or build or fix things? Use that ability to help someone out or bless someone's life. Has He blessed you with a home? Invite people into it. A car? Use it to go visit someone. A job? Reach out to your coworkers. He does not bless us so that we can hide away our blessings, keeping them to ourselves, stacking them up in the corners higher and higher, hoarding them for our own happiness. I'm not saying that God doesn't want us to be happy or that His blessings aren't for us to enjoy. Of course, He blesses us because He loves us. He has blessed us abundantly, so much so, that we could never hope to repay Him. The gift of salvation and eternity with Him should never be taken for granted; we owe Him everything. A. W. Tozer, in his book *The Missing Jewel*, eloquently expresses how God has given us so much more than we could ever hope to repay.

> Sometimes, I go to God and say, "God, if Thou dost never answer another prayer while I live on this earth, I will still worship Thee as long as I live and in the ages to come for what Thou hast done already." God's already put me so far in debt that if I were to live one million millenniums I couldn't pay Him for what He's done for me.[44]

We, who have been so richly blessed, should, in turn, attempt to be a vessel through whom God can bless those around us. Hopefully, those God blesses through us will be encouraged to bless someone else in their life and the chain will continue. This is how we bear fruit for God.

In Matthew 10, Jesus is sending out the twelve apostles to teach. After giving them authority to heal the sick and demon-possessed, he reminds them, "Freely you received, freely give" (Matthew 10:8).

---

[44] A. W. Tozer, *Worship: The Missing Jewel* (Heritage Series, Christian Publications, 1992), 24.

He was saying that they had been given power to heal and cast out demons, so don't be stingy with sharing it. This is good for us to remember as well, and it doesn't only mean giving money. This passage isn't talking about money. Jesus is saying that "What I have given you, I gave to you freely"; so freely give to others out of that abundance. In Acts 3, Peter and John are going into the temple when they come across a lame man asking for money. Peter's response was not to give him money, because Peter didn't have any money to give, but he gave the man something of much greater value.

> Now Peter and John were going up to the temple at the ninth hour, the hour of prayer. And a man who had been lame from his mother's womb was being carried along, whom they used to set down every day at the gate of the temple which is called Beautiful, in order to beg alms of those who were entering the temple. When he saw Peter and John about to go into the temple, he began asking to receive alms. But Peter, along with John, fixed his gaze on him and said, "Look at us!" And he began to give them his attention, expecting to receive something from them. But Peter said, "I do not possess silver and gold, but what I do have I give to you: In the name of Jesus Christ the Nazarene—walk!" And seizing him by the right hand, he raised him up; and immediately his feet and his ankles were strengthened. With a leap he stood upright and began to walk; and he entered the temple with them, walking and leaping and praising God. And all the people saw him walking and praising God; and they were taking note of him as being the one who used to sit at the Beautiful Gate of the temple to beg alms, and they were filled with wonder and amazement at what had happened to him. (Acts 3:1–10)

We who have been saved by the grace of God, through Jesus our Lord, have been given a great gift—a relationship with the Creator of the universe! "Freely you have received; freely give!" Kindness and goodness are gifts of the Holy Spirit, given to us who believe. The purpose of these gifts is to bless the people He puts in our path. To share this saving grace with those who are lost is our highest calling. To be kind and good to those around us, sacrificing our own selfishness and reaching out to those in need. These actions open doors and soften hearts and make a path for the gospel to enter in. When we are kind to fellow Christians, we strengthen and encourage their faith and spur them on to good works as well. So then, in whatever God has given you—whether money, time, skill, or ability—use it to bless others. In this way, we become the fruitful garden that God desires, for a garden does not exist for its own sake, but it fulfills the purpose of the Master Gardener.

> Let us not lose heart in doing good, for in due time we will reap if we do not grow weary. So then, while we have opportunity, let us do good to all people, and especially to those who are of the household of the faith. (Galatians 6:9–10)

Questions to Consider

Chapter 10: Kindness and Goodness

1. In what ways can kindness and goodness be self-serving?

   _____

   _____

   _____

   _____

   _____

2. Think of a time when you may have hoarded the blessings of God. Briefly describe it.

   _____

   _____

   _____

   _____

   _____

3. What is the greatest blessing that God has given us?

   _____

   _____

   _____

   _____

   _____

4. List several ways that you can show kindness or goodness in the name of Jesus this week. Commit to at least one of them.

   _____

   _____

   _____

   _____

   _____

Using the lines below, write out Hebrews 13:6. Reread it many times during the week. Try to commit it to memory.

_____
_____
_____
_____
_____
_____
_____
_____
_____
_____
_____
_____
_____
_____
_____
_____
_____
_____
_____
_____
_____
_____
_____
_____
_____
_____

Holy God,

Thank You for all the many blessings You have lavished on us. Show us how to be kind to those people You put in our path. Help us to never grow tired of doing good. In Jesus's name, amen.

CHAPTER 11

Faithfulness

Long-term goals are like planting a tree that will bear fruits
only after a few years. These trees take a long time to grow
but they provide lasting benefits. Unlike the seasonal crop
that gives you benefits only once, the trees keep bearing
fruit year after year without much effort. However, you
have to constantly work for a couple of years even when no
fruit is in sight. You must have faith and the motivation to
be able to put in continuous effort for a long time.[45]

—Awdhesh Singh

Now faith is confidence in what we hope for
and assurance about what we do not see.
This is what the ancients were commended for…
These were all commended for their faith,
yet none of them received what had been promised,
since God had planned something better for us
so that only together with us would they be made perfect.

—Hebrews 11:1–2, 39–40 (NIV)

When watching our garden grow and thrive, I am reminded of the
faithfulness of God. We prepare the soil and plant the seeds, and
they grow. We don't cause them to grow and bear fruit—they just
do it because that is what they were designed to do by their Creator.
They are true to their roots. If we plant a carrot seed, we don't get

---

[45] Awdhesh Singh, *31 Ways to Happiness* (Wisdom Tree, March 15, 2019).

an onion; we get a carrot. Our pear tree will not produce apples, nor will our plum tree produce peaches. God has designed each one to bear its own fruit, and so it is with all believers. We must be true to our roots—faithful to our Lord and Creator—to fulfill His purpose. Then we will bear the fruit He has designed each of us to bear.

To be faithful is to be true, committed, and sure. Faith is putting God as our foundation. He is the base upon which we build our lives. In Hebrews 11:1, we find the Bible's definition of *faith*. "Now faith is the assurance of things hoped for; the conviction of things not seen." Faith is knowing, with absolute assurance, that the word of God is true and inerrant. We are to be "all-in" and totally convinced that God is Who He says He is and that Jesus is Divine—God in the flesh, that He died and rose again and, in so doing, demolished sin and the power of the evil one. Often, we define *faith* as "belief." We believe in God and in Jesus Christ. Belief is a conscious acknowledgment of something—to accept something as true. But biblical belief and faith are deeper than mere acknowledgment. When demon-possessed people approached Jesus, they fell at His feet, acknowledging His authority. They recognized Him as divine. They believed in Him. The Bible tells us that the "demons believe and shudder" (James 2:19). So obviously saving faith involves a deeper sentiment than this. James goes on to say, regarding Abraham's faith and obedience: "You see that faith was working with his works, and as a result of the works, faith was perfected" (James 2:22). Faith is believing but a belief that is coupled with affection and devotion, knowing who God is, in His three persons, loving Him with our heart, soul, mind, and strength. This is not a passive stance. Too often, I have heard pastors and preachers teach that all you have to do to be saved is believe. Simply acknowledge that Jesus is real, and you're good to go. But I believe that this is not the truth of the Scriptures. It must go deeper than that. Don't misunderstand me; the Bible is true, and every word is to be believed. There are many verses in the Bible affirming that belief leads to salvation. Here are just a few of them:

> They said, "Believe in the Lord Jesus, and you
> will be saved, you and your household." And they

spoke the word of the Lord to him together with all who were in his house. And he took them that very hour of the night and washed their wounds, and immediately he was baptized, he and all his household. And he brought them into his house and set food before them, and rejoiced greatly, having believed in God with his whole household. (Acts 16:31–34)

But what does it say? "THE WORD IS NEAR YOU, IN YOUR MOUTH AND IN YOUR HEART"—that is, the word of faith which we are preaching, that if you confess with your mouth Jesus as Lord, and believe in your heart that God raised Him from the dead, you will be saved; for with the heart a person believes, resulting in righteousness, and with the mouth he confesses, resulting in salvation. (Romans 10:8–10)

In hope against hope he (Abraham) believed, so that he might become a father of many nations according to that which had been spoken, "SO SHALL YOUR DESCENDANTS BE." Without becoming weak in faith he contemplated his own body, now as good as dead since he was about a hundred years old, and the deadness of Sarah's womb; yet, with respect to the promise of God, he did not waver in unbelief but grew strong in faith, giving glory to God, and being fully assured that what God had promised, He was able also to perform. Therefore IT WAS ALSO CREDITED TO HIM AS RIGHTEOUSNESS. Now not for his sake only was it written that it was credited to him, but for our sake also, to whom it will be credited, as those who believe in Him who raised Jesus our Lord from the dead, He who was delivered over because of our transgressions, and was raised because of our justification. (Romans 4:18–25)

These verses clearly state that if we believe in the Lord Jesus Christ, we will be saved, that our belief is credited as righteousness. But the Bible also states that the demons believe and shudder. So are the demons saved? No. So what is the difference? In my understanding, it comes down to one word—*Lord*. If we believe in the *Lord*, we will be saved. What does it mean for Jesus to be Lord? It is more than just an acknowledgment of Him. According to Hebrews 11:1, it is an assurance and a conviction—this is more than just a passive acknowledgment. For Him to be our Lord means that we have surrendered our will to Him. We are allowing the Spirit to rule in our hearts. There's no going back. We are committed to His word and willing to live a life that is surrendered to His will. John MacArthur put it this way in his book *The Gospel According to Jesus*:

> Grace does not grant permission to live in the flesh; it supplies power to live in the Spirit… We have no business preaching grace to people who do not understand the implications of God's law. It is meaningless to expound on grace to someone who does not know the divine demand for righteousness. Those who do not even sense their own guilt cannot possibly comprehend God's mercy. You cannot preach a gospel of grace to someone who has not heard that God requires obedience and punishes disobedience.[46]

This is so very important, and we all need to take it to heart. Faithfulness is not just an acknowledgment of God and Jesus Christ. It is an understanding that we are lost without Him—that He, through His amazing gift of grace, has given us His Righteousness, which covers our sin and makes us pure and perfect in God's sight.

---

[46] John MacArthur, *The Gospel According to Jesus* (Zondervan, 2008).

We have laid our lives in His hand, allowing Him to be our Sovereign King. We relinquish our own authority and give Him everything. We read His word and obey it with our whole heart. We don't just accept His grace and walk away; that is not faith. Grace is too great a gift to be treated in that way. In his book *The Cost of Discipleship*, Dietrich Bonhoeffer differentiates between true grace, which he calls costly grace, and a shallow substitution, which he calls cheap grace.

> Cheap grace means grace sold on the market like cheapjacks' wares. The sacraments, the forgiveness of sin, and the consolations of religion are thrown away at cut prices. Grace is represented as the Church's inexhaustible treasury, from which she showers blessings with generous hands without asking questions or fixing limits. Grace without price; grace without cost! The essence of grace, we suppose, is that the account has been paid in advance; and because it has been paid, everything can be had for nothing. Since the cost was infinite, the possibilities of using and spending it are infinite. What would grace be if it were not cheap?
>
> Cheap grace is the preaching of forgiveness without requiring repentance, baptism without church discipline, Communion without confession, absolution without personal confession. Cheap grace is grace without discipleship, grace without the cross, grace without Jesus Christ, living and incarnate.
>
> Costly grace is the treasure hidden in the field; for the sake of it a man will go and sell all that he has. It is the pearl of great price to buy which the merchant will sell all his goods. It is the kingly rule of Christ, for whose sake a man will pluck out the eye which causes him to stum-

ble; it is the call of Jesus Christ at which the dis-
ciple leaves his nets and follows him.

Costly grace is the gospel which must be
sought again and again, the gift which must be
asked for, the door at which a man must knock.

Such grace is costly because it calls us to follow, and it is grace because it calls us to follow
Jesus Christ. It is costly because it costs a man his
life, and it is grace because it gives a man the only
true life. It is costly because it condemns sin, and
grace because it justifies the sinner. Above all, it is
costly because it cost God the life of his Son: "ye
were bought at a price," and what has cost God
much cannot be cheap for us. Above all, it is grace
because God did not reckon his Son too dear a
price to pay for our life, but delivered him up for
us. Costly grace is the Incarnation of God. [47]

When Jesus called the apostles, they immediately dropped what
they were doing and followed Him. They did not merely acknowledge Him and go back to fishing. They dropped their nets, left their
dad with the boat, and followed Jesus. Our response to Him should
be the same. We leave behind whatever we were about in our old life
and follow Him into a new and resurrected life. We are saved by the
generous gift of God's grace. He saves us from our sins and restores
us into a perfect relationship with Him. He gives us His Spirit to
guide and direct our lives. In return, we give Him all that we are
or ever hope to be. There is no call for selfishly walking away, as if
His grace were somehow due to us. We did nothing to earn it. We
are deplorably guilty, undeniably unworthy; but He loves us in spite
of that and restores us and makes us clean and holy in His sight.
Why would we choose to continue to live in the sin and ugliness of
self-absorbed self-righteousness? He has freed us from that life and

[47] Dietrich Bonhoeffer, *The Cost of Discipleship* (New York, London, Toronto, Sydney: Touchstone, Simon & Schuster), © 1959 by SCM Press Ltd.

set us free to live a life of faith, fully surrendered to our amazing and awesome God! How powerful and on fire the church would be if all God's people lived in surrendered faith, allowing His Spirit to guide us through every day!

The comparison of simple acknowledgment of Christ versus committing our lives to Him is an important concept to grasp. It is good for us to understand what is meant by God when He says to believe. Years ago, I heard a sermon in which the speaker gave a good analogy comparing faith to a bridge.[48]

You are being pursued by a fierce beast, and you are frantically trying to escape. You come to a deep cavern; thousands of feet below are jagged rocks and a deep, raging river. Your only escape is to get across the cavern before the beast overtakes you. You look up and see two bridges. The first is made of fraying, thin rope, with rotting wood planks. Some of the ropes have already given way, leaving the bridge tilted and dangling at a precarious angle. There are large gaps in the floor of the bridge where sections are falling away. It sways back and forth with the slightest breeze; not even the birds will trust their weight to it. The other bridge is solid, constructed of steel and concrete, massive and strong. Which bridge do you choose to believe in? You can put a huge amount of faith into the flimsy, rickety bridge and still wind up at the bottom of the cavern because that bridge, in spite of your faith, cannot carry you across. Instead, you approach the other bridge: the solid one. Again, you have a few choices. You can acknowledge that, yes, indeed, this is definitely a bridge. You can believe that it is a bridge, but that is not enough to save you from the approaching beast. Secondly, you can see that other people are escaping the beast by crossing over on this bridge. You can praise the Bridge Builder and Designer for making such a great Bridge, but still the beast comes for you. Or lastly, you can step out onto that strong and secure Bridge and walk across it, escaping the pursuing danger and enter a place of security and peace.

---

[48] Unfortunately, I don't remember the name of the speaker to give him credit. I had jotted the analogy into the margin of my Bible and ran across it again as I was studying.

As Jesus said, even faith as small as a mustard seed can accomplish great things if that faith is placed on the right Bridge. Jesus is that Bridge. If we keep our feet firmly planted in this world and refuse to leave it behind in order to step out onto the Bridge, then how can we be saved? Saving faith, saving belief, means you're all in, committed; your old self is dead, and you now walk a new life of faith in Jesus Christ.

I heard another faith analogy from an African missionary named Ronald who, years ago, visited the summer youth camp where I was working. The campers were gathered around the campfire after dark, staring into the dancing flames. The missionary moved close to the fire and began to speak. He took hold of a piece of wood on the outer edge of the fire and held it up. He explained how, even though the tip of the log was burning, the wood was still cool enough to pick it up and remove it from the fire. Very soon, the fire at the tip smoldered out. He warned that Satan wants to pull us away from God, to take us out of the fire. If we are lukewarm or hanging out on the edges, then Satan has an advantage. Then the missionary moved the campers' focus to the very core of the fire, deep in under the wood—a bright, glowing, red-hot presence, hotter even than the flames. He asked them, "Where is the wood at the center? Can you see where the wood ends and the fire begins? No, the wood and the fire are one. There is no separating them. If you reached in with a pair of tongs and tried to remove a chunk, it would either crumble and remain in the fire or continue to burn until all the wood was consumed." This is the faith we need to have. To be so on fire for God that He indwells us completely and our old self is no longer discernible. We are changed to be like Him; Satan cannot get a grip on us or remove us from His hand.

Our faith is weak and often small. But Jesus teaches us that it is not the amount of faith we have but where we have placed that faith. Even a faith that seems small and impotent, when placed in the hands of Almighty God, can accomplish much. Faithful—to be full of faith, full of conviction, full of assurance, filled with belief—this is what it means to have faith; and it is through our faith that grace is realized. It doesn't mean that we are flawless or that we will never struggle with our desires to follow the world, but it does mean that God's great love for us will always pursue us and call us back to Him. A. W. Tozer expressed this thought beautifully:

> O God, I have tasted Thy goodness, and it has both satisfied me and made me thirsty for more. I am painfully conscious of my need for further grace. I am ashamed of my lack of desire. O God, the Triune God, I want to want Thee; I long to be filled with longing; I thirst to be made more thirsty still. Show me Thy glory, I pray Thee, so that I may know Thee indeed. Begin in mercy a new work of love within me. Say to my soul, "Rise up my love, my fair one, and come away." Then give me grace to rise and follow Thee up from this misty lowland where I have wandered so long. Amen.[49]

Isn't this the longing of our hearts as well? Our spirits long to be in communion with His Spirit. This is faith: to be totally in love with Him and committed to His will in our lives willing to obey whatever He has asked us to do, even if it goes against what society says is popular or expected. According to *Vine's Expository Dictionary of Biblical Words*, "The main elements in 'Faith' in its relation to the invisible God...are (1) A firm conviction, producing a full acknowledgement of God's revelation or truth; (2) A personal surrender to Him; (3) A conduct inspired by such surrender."[50] God is God. If the world says one thing and God says another, then simply the world is wrong and God is right. That seems like such a simple concept, and yet many Christians struggle with putting it into action. We try to twist the Scriptures to say what we want them to say, or we simply leave out the parts that bother us. But true faith puts God on the throne and

---

[49] A. W. Tozer, *The Pursuit of God: The Human Thirst for the Divine*, (Bethany House, 2013), 3.

[50] W. E. Vine, *Vine's Expository Dictionary of Biblical Words* (Thomas Nelson Publishers, 1985), 222.

allows Him to rule. His word is truth—all of it—even the parts that are hard to swallow. True faith means loving God completely and giving Him our whole heart, soul, mind, and strength. This goes far beyond simple acknowledgment; this faith is deep and enduring, down to the roots. So, like the garden plants, we must be true to our roots, for He who planted us is faithful.

> Therefore having been justified by faith, we have peace with God through our Lord Jesus Christ, through whom also we have obtained our introduction by faith into this grace in which we stand; and we exult in hope of the glory of God. (Romans 5:1–2)

Questions to Consider

Chapter 11: Faithfulness

1. What is the definition of faith?

_____
_____
_____
_____
_____

2. How do you define saving belief or saving faith in Jesus Christ?

_____
_____
_____
_____
_____

3. What does it mean for Jesus to be the Lord of your life?

_____
_____
_____
_____
_____

4. What is the difference between cheap grace and costly grace?

_____
_____
_____
_____

5. Is it bad to have a small amount of faith? Explain.

_____
_____
_____
_____
_____

Using the lines below, write out Hebrews 11:1. Reread it many times during the week. Try to commit it to memory.

_____

_____

_____

_____

_____

_____

_____

_____

_____

_____

_____

_____

_____

_____

_____

_____

_____

_____

_____

_____

_____

_____

_____

_____

_____

Our Father,

Help us to grow in our faith and to believe in You more. Thank You for Your faithfulness to us and Your amazing grace toward us who believe. In Jesus's name, amen.

CHAPTER 12

Gentleness

Gentleness is not weakness. Just the opposite. Preserving a
gentle spirit in a heartless world takes extraordinary courage,
determination, and resilience. Do not underestimate the
power of gentleness because gentleness is strength wrapped
in peace, and therein lies the power to change the world.[51]

—L. R. Knost

Relating to God as the heart of tenderness identifies the Holy
Spirit as the bond of tenderness between the Father and the Son.
Thus, the gentle Spirit dwelling within us is the deepest expression
of tenderness—indeed, the Spirit-filled Christian is one whose heart
is overflowing with tenderness—and it represents
the full healing of our pain through his coming to us.[52]

—Brennan Manning

When working in the garden, often brute force is required to pull
large, dead roots from the soil or to turn over cold, hard ground; but
at other times, a soft touch is needed. Whether it is planting fragile
seedlings or training a tender vine to grow in a certain direction, a
gentle hand is necessary for these more delicate jobs. The leather
gloves come off so we can feel what we're doing, being sensitive to
the fragility of the plants. Occasionally, we have discovered injured

---

[51] L. R. Knost, *Two Thousand Kisses a Day: Gentle Parenting through the Ages and Stages* (Little Hearts Books, LLC, February 20, 2013).

[52] Brennan Manning, *The Wisdom of Tenderness* (Harper One, October 12, 2010), 23–24, E-book.

birds in our garden. Recently, a pygmy owl flew into a window that overlooks the garden, knocking himself out. Pygmy owls are small enough to fit in the palm of my hand. I picked him up and saw he was still breathing. I gently held him and spoke quietly to him, stroking his feathers. Eventually, he woke up and just sat in my hand for several minutes while he recovered, all the while sinking his very sharp talons into my palm. After a few minutes, he flew away. My gentleness with this little bird had nothing to do with my strength but had everything to do with peace and control.

Gentleness is not a popular character trait in the world today. Many people equate it with being weak or lacking conviction. But that is far from the truth. To be gentle means that we have the capacity or even the inclination to be harsh, overbearing, critical, or impatient; but we choose not to be. This is not weakness but strength. It takes strength and conviction to rein in negative attitudes. In the garden, obviously I have the strength to break a branch off a plant or tear it, roots and all, from the ground. Gentleness means I am in control of my strength, so I can handle the delicate plants without damaging them.

Gentleness is strength under control, and its benefactors are the people we come into contact with. Gentleness benefits the people around us. It helps them grow. This is such an important aspect of strength. Without gentleness, a person becomes an unapproachable wall. We all can think of someone like this, who is inflexible and demands that everything be their way, who pushes their way into conversations or who forces their opinions onto others, with no thought as to how their actions might affect the people around them. To lack gentleness is to be self-centered, because this type of person is only concerned about showing their own strength. Ecclesiastes 3 tells us that there is a time for everything under heaven, "a time to plant and a time to uproot what is planted" (Ecclesiastes 3:2). Planting requires gentleness, while uprooting requires strength. We need a balance between the two. We should not be people who are constantly uprooting and never planting. Henry Wadsworth Longfellow, an American poet from the 1800s, wrote a lovely poem entitled "The Village Blacksmith," where he describes in detail the strength of the blacksmith, his strong and rugged hands, brawny arms, and muscles of iron. Later in the poem, he tells how the blacksmith hears his daughter singing in church and wipes the tears away with his rugged and rough hand. In this poem, Longfellow vividly portrays the strength of the blacksmith and the tenderness of a father and husband all wrapped up in one man.

"The Village Blacksmith"
by Henry Wadsworth Longfellow

Under a spreading chestnut-tree
    The village smithy stands;
The smith, a mighty man is he,
With large and sinewy hands,
And the muscles of his brawny arms
Are strong as iron bands.
His hair is crisp, and black, and long;
His face is like the tan;
His brow is wet with honest sweat,
He earns whate'er he can,
And looks the whole world in the face,
For he owes not any man.
Week in, week out, from morn till night,
You can hear his bellows blow;
You can hear him swing his heavy sledge,
With measured beat and slow,
Like a sexton ringing the village bell,
When the evening sun is low.
And children coming home from school
Look in at the open door;
They love to see the flaming forge,
And hear the bellows roar,
And catch the burning sparks that fly
Like chaff from a threshing-floor.
He goes on Sunday to the church,
And sits among his boys;

He hears the parson pray and preach,
He hears his daughter's voice
Singing in the village choir,
And it makes his heart rejoice.
It sounds to him like her mother's voice
Singing in Paradise!
He needs must think of her once more,
How in the grave she lies;
And with his hard, rough hand he wipes
A tear out of his eyes.
Toiling,—rejoicing,—sorrowing,
Onward through life he goes;
Each morning sees some task begin,
Each evening sees it close;
Something attempted, something done,
Has earned a night's repose.
Thanks, thanks to thee, my worthy friend,
For the lesson thou hast taught!
Thus at the flaming forge of life
Our fortunes must be wrought;
Thus on its sounding anvil shaped
Each burning deed and thought.[53]

This poem beautifully expresses the combination of strength and gentleness in the blacksmith. His obvious strength and physical fortitude were seen by everyone who passed by his forge. But his strength did not govern his heart. He was still touched by his daughter's voice singing in the church choir, reminding him of his late wife and bringing tears to his eyes. What a sweet and eloquent depiction of strength and gentleness woven together.

Strength is a positive characteristic. It is good to be "strong in the Lord and in the strength of His might" (Ephesians 6:10). Joshua was also instructed to be "strong and courageous" (Joshua 1:9).

---

[53] Henry Wadsworth Longfellow, *The Village Blacksmith*, Poets.org: Academy of American Poets, New York, accessed February 4, 2021, Public Domain USA.

Strength is wonderful and should not be discouraged. At times, our society tries to tell us that strength (especially in men) is a negative. that men should be wimpy and passive. I believe this comes from the prevalence of domestic abuse in many homes. It is often assumed that a strong man must be an abusive man or a domineering husband. On the other hand, if a man is gentle, society tends to label him as effeminate and lacking strength. Perhaps, this is why many men in our society are confused about their place. But this shows a lack of understanding of what it means to be gentle and strong. You cannot be gentle without strength, because gentleness is strength under control. A man who is strong—especially strong in the Lord—demands respect, not that he insists on it, but his character attracts respect. When this kind of man treats people with gentleness and gentle words, it is deeply meaningful. It brings to my mind the image of a Kung Fu master who gently passes his wisdom on to a child, or a strong man gently holding his infant child. Power and strength under control—this is what it means to be gentle. I enjoy watching veterinarian shows on TV where the doc goes out to the farm to try to save a dying calf. The farmer—rugged, strong, and all business—is shown cradling the little baby cow with tears running down his face. Another episode showed a big, burly tough guy struggling to hold back the tears as he held his injured kitty. These are touching examples of strength and tenderness knitted together.

But it is not just men who need guidance in understanding gentleness. The women's fight for equality has caused many women to grow up with an attitude that they are tough as nails and that gentleness is somehow a weakness. In 1 Peter 3, Peter gives instructions to women.

> In the same way, you wives, be submissive to your own husbands so that even if any of them are disobedient to the word, they may be won without a word by the behavior of their wives, as they observe your chaste and respectful behavior. Your adornment must not be merely external—braiding the hair, and wearing gold jewelry, or putting

on dresses; but let it be the hidden person of the
heart, with the imperishable quality of a gentle
and quiet spirit, which is precious in the sight of
God. (1 Peter 3:1–4)

In today's progressive views, this verse is not warmly welcomed.
Many people just choose to pass it by, but God's words should never
be passed by. Peter is not saying that women should be weak or shut
down. Submission, like gentleness, is power and strength under control. Women are strong and very capable, able to multitask, run a
house full of children, hold down a job, cook, clean, organize, and
more. All of this requires great strength. Our society tells us that
women can accomplish anything, that they are strong and indepen-
dent. This is undoubtedly true; however, this can produce women
who become overbearing and even downright mean to other women
and also to the men in their lives. They feel they don't need anyone's
help, because they are capable without anyone. They are offended if a
man even holds the door open for them. This causes many women to
become demanding and demeaning to the people around them. This
kind of strength is self-serving; it does not consider the other person.
I don't need my husband to open doors for me or hold the car door
while I get in the car. I don't need him to defrost my car windows on
a frosty morning or build a fire in the fireplace. I don't need him to
put himself between me and the traffic when we are walking. I am
perfectly capable of doing all these things on my own. So why do I
allow him to do them? Because I love him, and he wants to do these
things for me. So I submit, holding back my strength and allowing
him to be strong. This is for his benefit, not mine. God calls us to be
gentle, to control our strength so as not to harm the people around
us. We are more effective at bearing fruit when we are gentle, and this
is precious in God's sight.

James tells us that gentleness is a characteristic of wisdom.
Gentleness is not rooted in selfish ambition; on the contrary, selfish

ambition leads to chaos and every evil thing. But God's wisdom is gentle and peaceful.

> Who among you is wise and understanding? Let him show by his good behavior his deeds in the gentleness of wisdom. But if you have bitter jealousy and selfish ambition in your heart, do not be arrogant and so lie against the truth. This wisdom is not that which comes down from above, but is earthly, natural, demonic. For where jealousy and selfish ambition exist, there is disorder and every evil thing. But the wisdom from above is first pure, then peaceable, gentle, reasonable, full of mercy and good fruits, unwavering, without hypocrisy. And the seed whose fruit is righteousness is sown in peace by those who make peace. (James 3:13–18)

God calls us to be strong and unwavering in our faith; and coupled with this strength is gentleness, the ability to rein in our urge to condemn or criticize or control the people around us. This leads us to the final fruit of the Spirit: self-control.

Questions to Consider

Chapter 12: Gentleness

1. Why is gentleness sometimes viewed as an unpopular trait in today's society?

_____

_____

_____

_____

_____

2. In what ways are strength and gentleness connected?

_____

_____

_____

_____

_____

3. Give an example of a time when you held back your strength and acted with gentleness?

_____

_____

_____

_____

_____

4. In what way is God's wisdom gentle (James 3:13–18)?

_____

_____

_____

_____

_____

Using the lines below, write out James 3:17–18. Reread it many times during the week. Try to commit it to memory.

_____
_____
_____
_____
_____
_____
_____
_____
_____
_____
_____
_____
_____
_____
_____
_____
_____
_____
_____
_____
_____
_____
_____
_____
_____

Father God,

Help us to learn how to be strong in Your might while maintaining an attitude of gentleness.
In Jesus's name, amen.

CHAPTER 13

Self-Control

You can't always control the wind, but you can control your sails.
—Author Unknown

Do you not know that those who run in a race all run,
but only one receives the prize? Run in
such a way that you may win.
Everyone who competes in the games
exercises self-control in all things.
They then do it to receive a perishable wreath,
but we an imperishable. Therefore I run in such a way,
as not without aim; I box in such a way, as not beating the air;
but I discipline my body and make it my slave,
so that, after I have preached to others,
I myself will not be disqualified.
—1 Corinthians 9:24–27

Self-control among the garden plants is unheard of. Plants and trees do not demonstrate self-control. On the contrary, if left to their own devices, they will either die or go wild and take over the whole garden. In the Pacific Northwest, we are often plagued by wild blackberries. If there is a piece of ground, no matter how large or small, blackberry vines will appear. Although the fruit is quite tasty, the vines can become a burden as they invade the yard. No matter how many vines you pull up, chop up, poison, or burn, it is inevitable that they will return. Sometimes, I think that the entire state of Oregon has one massive blackberry root system running under the surface.

If left unchecked, these vines will take over. Plants allowed to take over the garden can kill other plants and often are not fruitful as their nutrients are striving to keep alive the rambling vines instead of nourishing the fruit. Sometimes, people give up trying to fight the blackberries and become content simply to maintain them and confine them to a certain area, but inevitably, they won't stay in that designated spot, and the people must continue to fight them back. In the same way, Christians who are not guided by the Spirit of God will die spiritually or go off in their own direction, leading many people astray, following after a gospel that is not from God, or seeking earthly treasures instead of the eternal. Branches that are not pruned and tended will break with the winter wind, ice, and snow—just as Christians who are not controlled by the Spirit will buckle under when hard times come. Diseased plants will die and spread their disease to healthy plants without the hands of the Gardener to heal and cut away the dead and dying. Similarly, churches and individuals who are not led by the Spirit will eventually spread this false spirituality to their followers. Some churches just give up trying to eradicate false doctrines and allow them to remain, thinking that they can somehow control them and keep them from spreading. But just like the blackberry vines, false doctrine, if allowed to remain, will continue to spread and infect the church. Without the guiding hand of the Master Gardener, these churches and their followers will die spiritually. It is essential that we allow the Spirit of God to guide, prune, and direct us. This is why self-control is a fruit of the Spirit—it is not something that we are good at on our own. We need the Spirit's help to attain it.

The first character trait in the list of the fruits of the Spirit is love—which is the most important commandment in the Bible; the last in the list is self-control, which is possibly the most difficult for many of us to achieve. In fact, all of the other fruits previously discussed rely on love and self-control to some degree: joy, peace, patience, kindness, goodness, faithfulness, gentleness. Without love and self-control, it would be difficult, if not impossible, to reach these goals. These two traits are the bookends of the fruits of the Spirit, and the rest are dependent upon them. Self-control is difficult. It does not come naturally, but the Spirit of God within believers gives us the power and conviction to achieve it. Second Timothy 1:7 states, "For the Spirit God gave us does not make us timid, but gives us power, love and self-discipline" (NIV).

According to *Merriam-Webster*, *self-control* is defined as "restraint exercised over one's own impulses, emotions or desires."[54] The opposite of self-control would be indulgence, which means a person is practicing no restraint on their impulses, emotions, or desires. Indulgence is something that makes us feel good, whether or not it is good for us or beneficial to those around us. The Spirit gives us the gift of self-control. Indulgence does not come from the Spirit of God but from the world and our fleshly desires. To be led by the Spirit of God is to put to death our worldly desires and set our minds on God. This problem of self-control is nothing new; Christians throughout the ages have striven with this. To quote again from Romans 7, where Paul is troubling over this struggle for self-control.

> For what I am doing, I do not understand; for I am not practicing what I would like to do, but I am doing the very thing I hate... For the good that I want, I do not do, but I practice the very evil that I do not want. But if I am doing the very thing I do not want, I am no longer the one doing it, but sin which dwells in me. (Romans 7:15, 19–20)

In Paul's letter to the Galatians, he again explains the battle between the fleshly nature and the Spirit. And it is in this passage that he lists the fruits of the Spirit, as well as many of the deeds of the flesh.

> But I say, walk by the Spirit, and you will not carry out the desire of the flesh. For the flesh

---

[54] "Self-control." *Merriam-Webster.com Dictionary.* Merriam-Webster, https://www.merriam-webster.com/dictionary/self-control. Accessed February 23, 2021.

sets its desire against the Spirit, and the Spirit against the flesh; for these are in opposition to one another, so that you may not do the things that you please. But if you are led by the Spirit, you are not under the Law. Now the deeds of the flesh are evident, which are: immorality, impurity, sensuality, idolatry, sorcery, enmities, strife, jealousy, outbursts of anger, disputes, dissensions, factions, envying, drunkenness, carousing, and things like these, of which I forewarn you, just as I have forewarned you, that those who practice such things will not inherit the kingdom of God. But the fruit of the Spirit is love, joy, peace, patience, kindness, goodness, faithfulness, gentleness, self-control; against such things there is no law. Now those who belong to Christ Jesus have crucified the flesh with its passions and desires. If we live by the Spirit, let us also walk by the Spirit. (Galatians 5:16–25)

The struggle for self-control is real, whether we are striving to control emotions, such as anger, fear, doubt, and frustration, or trying to control actions, such as talking when we should be silent or not giving in to our desires for self-gratification, whether that is drugs, alcohol, pornography, or eating that whole plate of cookies. We are all fighting this battle. Our natural tendency is to take care of ourselves first, to do what makes us feel good. This is evident even from infancy. A baby has no concern for how their crying affects their parents. All they know is that they need something, and so they cry until the need is met. As a child grows, they learn to control this demanding nature and hopefully develop traits such as kindness and patience and self-control. But even as adults, we continue to struggle with this. Why is abortion such a huge issue in our society? Why are murder rates and other crimes on the rise? These are a direct result of a lack of self-control and the desire to take care of our own needs without regard for the other persons involved.

I think we sometimes equate self-indulgence with freedom—to be free to do whatever we want, whenever we want. Let's take food for example. Sticking to a good eating plan doesn't always "feel" like freedom. It often feels more like a restriction. I can't have that brownie, because it's not on my plan. Self-indulgence, on the other hand, "feels" like freedom. Eat the brownie; go ahead, have another! It is easy to get caught in that trap because self-indulgence feels so free. But the reality is just the opposite. We are slaves to the one we obey. If we obey our indulgences, we are enslaved by them. And don't we see this all around us? Self-indulgence and a lack of self-control with regards to food leads to weight gain, obesity, diabetes, heart disease, joint issues, and shortened life span. We can see the prevalence of this in our society. I see it in my own mirror! This is not freedom but enslavement, and that is just talking about food. Our world lacks self-control in so many ways: drugs, alcohol, sex, pornography, abortion, domestic abuse, rage, child abuse, living outside our means, and the way we talk to people who disagree with us, to name just a few. This one trait of self-control, if mastered by our society, could go a long way toward creating a world of peace and unity.

But how do we overcome? There is only one way: we must die to ourselves and live for Christ Jesus—to allow His Spirit within us to guide and direct our path. It is a daily commitment and sometimes even a minute-by-minute commitment. John Piper wrote an article on this topic entitled *The Fierce Fruit of Self-Control*. Here is an excerpt from that article.

> Fundamental to the Christian view of self-control is that it is a gift. It is the fruit of the Holy Spirit: "The fruit of the Spirit is love, joy, peace... self-control" (Galatians 5:22–23). How do we "strive" against our fatal desires? Paul answers: "For this I toil, struggling [*agonizomenos*] with all his energy that he powerfully works within me" (Colossians 1:29). He "agonizes" by the power of Christ, not his own. Similarly, he tells us, "If by the Spirit you put to death the deeds of the body,

you will live" (Romans 8:13). "Not by might, nor by power, but by my Spirit, says the Lord of hosts" (Zechariah 4:6). We must be fierce! Yes. But not by our might. "The horse is made ready for the day of battle, but the victory belongs to the Lord. (Proverbs 21:31).

And how does the Spirit produce this fruit of self-control in us? By instructing us in the superior preciousness of grace, and enabling us to see and savor (that is, "trust") all that God is for us in Jesus. "The grace of God has appeared...training us to renounce...worldly passions...in the present age" (Titus 2:11–12). When we really see and believe that God is for us by grace through Jesus Christ, the power of wrong desires is broken. Therefore, the fight for self-control is a fight of faith. "Fight the good fight of the faith. Take hold of the eternal life to which you were called" (1 Timothy 6:12).[55]

When we feel weak, we call on the Spirit to strengthen us. We ask Him to help us, and He will. The Spirit of God gives us power to put to death the deeds of the body. It is not by our own strength, or we would have no hope. The Spirit of God gives us grace to overcome. This is a fight of faith, as Piper puts it. We have to put aside our indulgences and find our freedom in Christ. In Galatians 5:1, Paul gives us these words of encouragement: "It was for freedom that Christ set us free; therefore keep standing firm and do not be subject again to a yoke of slavery." Slavery is being obedient to the fleshly desires of this world, which leads to misery. Overindulgence and a lack of self-control eventually lead to pain, misery, and despair. If we have no self-control in our spending, we wind up in debt up to our

---

[55] Piper, John. *The Fierce Fruit of Self-Control.* Desiring God, May 15, 2001. Accessed February 6, 2021. <desiringGod.org>

eyeballs or bankrupt. If we have no self-control over drugs or alcohol, we become addicted, and nothing matters more than the next buzz. Rage and out-of-control anger have no good end; the same is true for abuse. All of these problems stem from self-gratification. They are self-centered indulgences. People engaged in these activities are not concerned about being loving or kind or good or faithful; they are only concerned with what they want or think they need. Child and spousal abuse would vanish if the abuser put the needs of their family ahead of their own. Abortion could be nearly eliminated if we thought more about the innocent child whose life is being ended, and less about our own inconvenience. Obesity would be greatly "reduced" if we listened more to the Spirit of God and less to the refrigerator. Every one of us is guilty here. I am talking to myself in this chapter because I struggle with this every day. We've discussed a few issues here, but each of us can fill in the blank with our own self-control struggles. God wants us to be free. When we live self-controlled lives, led by the Spirit of God, then we are free from the shackles of this world.

> If Christ is in you, though the body is dead because of sin, yet the spirit is alive because of righteousness. But if the Spirit of Him who raised Jesus from the dead dwells in you, He who raised Christ Jesus from the dead will also give life to your mortal bodies through His Spirit who dwells in you.
>
> So then, brethren, we are under obligation, not to the flesh, to live according to the flesh— for if you are living according to the flesh, you must die; but if by the Spirit you are putting to death the deeds of the body, you will live. For all who are being led by the Spirit of God, these are sons of God. (Romans 8:10–14)

In the garden, the Gardener prunes, ties up, guides, and directs the plants, enabling all of them to reach their fullest potential and produce the greatest harvest. In our lives, the Spirit gives us self-control. We have free choice, yes; but His Spirit within us gives us strength to control our fleshly nature and live by the fruits of the Spirit. Therefore, it seems appropriate that the final trait in the fruits of the Spirit is self-control, because mastering this one thing makes all the rest fall more easily into place. It is easier to love others, to be joyful, peaceable, kind and good, patient, faithful, and gentle when our self-indulgence is put aside; and we allow the Spirit of God to control us. In the verses immediately following the fruits of the Spirit in Galatians 5, Paul writes, "Now those who belong to Christ Jesus have crucified the flesh with its passions and desires. If we live by the Spirit, let us also walk by the Spirit" (Galatians 5:24–25).

Questions to Consider

Chapter 13: Self-Control

1. In what ways do love and self-control affect all the other fruits of the Spirit?

_____

_____

_____

_____

_____

2. How did Paul explain his struggle for self-control in Romans 7:15–8:2?

_____

_____

_____

_____

_____

3. Why does self-indulgence feel like freedom? Why is this not true?

_____

_____

_____

_____

_____

4. How do we develop self-control?

_____

_____

_____

_____

_____

Using the lines below, write out 1 Corinthians 9:26–27. Reread it many times during the week. Try to commit it to memory.

_____
_____
_____
_____
_____
_____
_____
_____
_____
_____
_____
_____
_____
_____
_____
_____
_____
_____
_____
_____
_____
_____
_____
_____

Holy God,

It is so easy for us to lose control of our fleshly nature. Give us strength and endurance to follow the leading of Your Spirit and not the desires of the flesh. In Jesus's name, amen.

CHAPTER 14

The Harvest

Now He who supplies seed to the sower and bread for food
will supply and multiply your seed for sowing and increase
the harvest of your righteousness; you will be enriched in
everything for all liberality, which through us is producing
thanksgiving to God. For the ministry of this service is not only
fully supplying the needs of the saints, but is also overflowing
through many thanksgivings to God. Because of the proof given
by this ministry, they will glorify God for your obedience to
your confession of the gospel of Christ and for the liberality of
your contribution to them and to all, while they also, by prayer
on your behalf, yearn for you because of the surpassing grace
of God in you. Thanks be to God for His indescribable gift!
—2 Corinthians 9:10–15

Jesus said to them, "My food is to do the will of Him who
sent Me and to accomplish His work. Do you not say,
'There are yet four months, and then comes the harvest'?
Behold, I say to you, lift up your eyes and look on the fields,
that they are white for harvest. Already he who reaps is
receiving wages and is gathering fruit for life eternal; so that
he who sows and he who reaps may rejoice together."
—John 4:34–36

The harvest—what an amazing and busy time! The second round of
raspberries are ripe—ready to pick and process into jam. Grapes are
heavy on the vine. Tomatoes are fat and red. Pears and apples weigh

down the branches. Pumpkins are showing off their bright-orange color. A variety of vegetables fill our baskets: onions, garlic, carrots, radishes, zucchini, and the peppers… The jalapeños are beautiful! Such an abundance! We cannot possibly use all this harvest. We can't keep it to ourselves; it would only spoil before we could use it, and then it would be lost. So we share it. We give to friends and family, to pantries who share with those in need. We make jam out of our abundance of berries, and we give it away. What a joy it is to share our abundance!

Is this not what we are called to do with all the gifts that God has given us? He has given us an abundance of blessings: His Son, His Spirit, His Word, His mercy, His righteousness, and His abundant grace that gives us salvation and eternal life with Him. In addition to all that, He has given us skills, talents, and abilities so that we can bless others and turn their eyes to Him. Everything He has given us we can share with those around us. To hoard the blessings of God, to keep them only for ourselves is incredibly selfish. Can we call ourselves Christlike if we bury our blessings in the sand? Why do we have the abilities and skills that we have? Is it a coincidence? Happenstance? Or is it by design? As Christians, we believe that God is in control. He gives gifts to each of us so that we can accomplish a purpose for Him. First Peter 4:10–11 states, "As each one has received a special gift, employ it in serving one another as good stewards of the manifold grace of God." And again, in Romans 12, Paul encourages us to use the gifts we have been given, and to exercise them according to the grace given to us by God. He has blessed each of us with just the right amount of talent. We don't require more or less than what He has given us.

> For through the grace given to me I say to everyone among you not to think more highly of himself than he ought to think; but to think so as to have sound judgment, as God has allotted to each a measure of faith. For just as we have many members in one body and all the members do not have the same function, so we, who are many,

> are one body in Christ, and individually members one of another. Since we have gifts that differ according to the grace given to us, each of us is to exercise them accordingly: if prophecy, according to the proportion of his faith; if service, in his serving; or he who teaches, in his teaching; or he who exhorts, in his exhortation; he who gives, with liberality; he who leads, with diligence; he who shows mercy, with cheerfulness. (Romans 12:5–8)

As a teacher, I often marveled when one of my students just seemed to have a natural ability for art or music or writing... Whatever the skill...with no real training, they just had a knack for it. Our skills and talents are not only due to our own practice and desire, but they are also created in us...for a reason. These are gifts built into the fabric of the person—given by God. Have you ever tried to learn something new and you just couldn't get it, but then something else you try totally clicks with you and you take off as if it were second nature? For example, I've never been gifted in math—it has always eluded me. No matter how hard I try to make sense of numbers, I just continue to struggle; it is not my strong suit. On the other hand, art is something I can definitely get into. I can draw, paint, craft...anything art related. I have no real training; it just comes naturally to me. I can spend years studying mathematics and get nowhere, but art is second nature. In similar fashion, each person in the body of Christ has gifts which help to build up and expand the church, to spread His love to a broken world. Each one of us has abilities that are unique to them, which God has given to us to enhance His kingdom.

In the garden, there are many different players that contribute to a fruitful and flourishing garden, many different jobs at work. One may be tempted to think that the only players are the gardener and the plants, but there is so much more. The gardener uses gardening tools to turn the soil and remove weeds. These come in all sizes and shapes, from trowels to shovels to wheelbarrows. Our garden shed is full of garden tools, each one for a unique purpose. The garden requires mulches and fertilizers to enrich the soil; pest control to keep away slugs, moles, and unfriendly bugs; water to keep the roots moist and growing; sunshine to warm the soil and encourage photosynthesis; bees and other helpful bugs and birds to pollinate the blossoms; bright and fragrant flowers to attract the pollinators to the garden; and a harvester to gather the ripe fruits and vegetables. All of these work together to create a bountiful harvest. Each piece is important. How successful would a garden be without water or pollinators or sunshine? Each player in the garden does what they are designed for, and the result is a harvest that overflows in abundance.

So it is in the body of Christ. Are you a trowel or a shovel? Get your hands into the soil of someone's heart, and get it ready for planting. How can you ready a person's heart for the gospel? Care for their needs, love them unconditionally, be available and approachable, talk to them, and show kindness to them. Then hopefully they will thank God for your kindness and open their heart to Him.

Maybe you are mulch or fertilizer. Your gift is enrichment, to add to a person's heart the richness of God's love and mercy, to introduce them to the God of grace. In this way, you build on the foundation that someone else may have already laid. You do this by being present in their lives and sharing all the wonderful ways that God has blessed us.

Perhaps your gift is pest-control, to drive away anything that might harm or lead people away from the truth of God's word, to protect people from false teachings that might uproot their faith. This is done through teaching or preaching, sharing the truth of God's word...even the difficult parts...with love and mercy. This doesn't have to be done from the pulpit in a paid position, but one-on-one with the people you are close to. We all need accountability, to have friends who will call us out and remind us of the truth.

Water is another important element in the garden. This is a person who refreshes and blesses the hearts of people and encourages those who are down. They lift up the brokenhearted by praying with them, sending notes or care packages, bringing a meal or caring for their needs. It can be as simple as an email or phone call to remind people that you love them and are thinking about them.

Where would a garden be without the sun? If you are a sunny person, you warm the hearts of people, encouraging and caring for them. Just as the sun encourages plants to release oxygen, so your caring for people encourages them to release love and light to others.

Maybe you are a pollinator, a bee or a bird, searching out possibilities for spreading the Word, perhaps through an act of service that benefits the body of Christ or through helping a neighbor in need or paying for someone's groceries in the name of Christ. The hope is that because of your actions, people will be brought closer to the knowledge of God and salvation.

Then there are the flowers. These are the ones who attract workers for the Lord, maybe because of their outgoing and sincere personality or their eloquence in presenting the word of God. They encourage the body of Christ to spread the *good news* as pollen spreads throughout the garden from plant to plant.

And finally, the harvesters, those who gather the fruit, who go into the world, preaching the gospel, baptizing, and teaching the word of God. Missionaries, preachers, and teachers…we are all called to this.

It is important that each member of God's family does his or her part, that we utilize the gifts He has given us. Whether we are planting a seed or watering it, our part is important. Bearing fruit is a group project. Each member of the group must do their part in order for the group to have a successful and bountiful harvest.

How important is bearing fruit? Is this a critical aspect of being a follower of Christ Jesus? Here are a few passages that speak to this issue:

> "Indeed, the axe is already laid at the root of the trees; so every tree that does not bear good fruit is cut down and thrown into the fire."
>
> And the crowds were questioning him, saying, "Then what shall we do?" And he would answer and say to them, "The man who has two

tunics is to share with him who has none; and he
who has food is to do likewise." (Luke 3:9–11)

This passage is telling us that we ought to be caring for the
needs of the people around us. In this way, we are bearing fruit for
God. A Christian who is not bearing fruit in one way or another is
in danger of being cut down and thrown into the fire. God's grace
covers those people who belong to Him. Bearing fruit is evidence
that we, in fact, do belong to Him.

> So every good tree bears good fruit, but the bad
> tree bears bad fruit. A good tree cannot produce
> bad fruit, nor can a bad tree produce good fruit.
> Every tree that does not bear good fruit is cut
> down and thrown into the fire. So then, you will
> know them by their fruits. (Matthew 7:17–20)

Jesus is telling us that bearing fruit is evidence of a Christian life.
As people devoted to Christ, who have died to sin and live to God,
we submit to His will; and His will is that we bear fruit. John the
Baptist was baptizing in the Jordan River when many of the Pharisees
and Sadducees came out to also be baptized by him. But he rebuked
them, calling them a "brood of vipers."

> But when he saw many of the Pharisees and
> Sadducees coming for baptism, he said to them,
> "You brood of vipers, who warned you to flee
> from the wrath to come? Therefore bear fruit in
> keeping with repentance; and do not suppose that
> you can say to yourselves, 'We have Abraham for
> our father'; for I say to you that from these stones
> God is able to raise up children to Abraham. The
> axe is already laid at the root of the trees; there-
> fore every tree that does not bear good fruit is
> cut down and thrown into the fire." (Matthew
> 3:7–10)

John rebukes the Pharisees and Sadducees because their attitude was prideful, thinking that they were Abraham's children and, therefore, they didn't need to repent or humble themselves in any way. John makes it clear that God can raise up children for Himself from among the Gentiles; He doesn't require pompous and proud Jewish leaders who refuse to repent. Notice here that John equates bearing fruit with repentance. The proud and arrogant attitude of the Pharisees and Sadducees was far from repentant. An unrepentant soul cannot effectively bear fruit for God, because they are not in submission to His will. John's main message to the world at that time was "Repent, for the kingdom of heaven is at hand" (Matthew 3:2). A humble and penitent heart is in a position of submission to God and is effective at bearing fruit for Him. Paul also urges us to bear fruit in Romans 7:

> Therefore my brethren, you also were made to die to the Law through the body of Christ, so that you might be joined to another, to Him who was raised from the dead, in order that we might bear fruit for God. For while we were in the flesh, the sinful passions, which were aroused by the Law, were at work in the members of our body to bear fruit for death. But now we have been released from the Law, having died to that by which we were bound, so that we serve in newness of the Spirit and not in oldness of the letter. (Romans 7:4–6)

We are joined with Christ, dwelling in Him and He in us, so that we can bear fruit. To live a life led by our sinful passions leads only to chaos and death. It is a life lived entirely for self-gratification, with no repentance or concern for the lost. We have been set free from that kind of life. Because of our repentance and faith in Jesus, we have been redeemed—saved and covered with the righteousness of Jesus Christ. We no longer live for our sinful nature but for God. His Spirit indwells us and guides us. God is love, and His desire is that all people be saved. Therefore, it is natural, if, indeed, we are in Christ, that we bear fruit. Paul in his letter to the Colossians writes:

> For this reason also, since the day we heard of it, we have not ceased to pray for you and to ask that you may be filled with the knowledge of His will in all spiritual wisdom and understanding, so that you will walk in a manner worthy of the Lord, to please Him in all respects, bearing fruit in every good work and increasing in the knowledge of God; strengthened with all power, according to His glorious might, for the attaining of all steadfastness and patience; joyously giving thanks to the Father, who has qualified us to share in the inheritance of the saints in Light. (Colossians 1:9–12)

Paul encourages the church in Colossi to "walk in a manner worthy of the Lord, and to please Him in all respects." What does it mean to do this? I believe that it means that God wants us to be humble, to be repentant, to remember that He alone is *sovereign* and we owe Him everything. We need to have an attitude and a posture that submits to His will. Paul then states that we should be bearing fruit for God and increasing in the knowledge of God. We need to study and understand the word of God, increasing in our knowledge. That is an ongoing thing. We don't ever arrive at the destination; we are constantly striving for more. This helps us to be more effective at bearing fruit. What follows next in the verse is a beautiful promise: that we will be strengthened with power…attaining steadfastness and patience…joyously giving thanks…and sharing in the inheritance of the saints in Light. What a wonderful promise! The Word of God is never to be taken lightly. It is living and active and constantly bears fruit for God. Earlier in the same chapter of Colossians, Paul wrote,

> We give thanks to God, the Father of our Lord Jesus Christ, praying always for you, since we

> heard of your faith in Christ Jesus and the love
> which you have for all the saints; because of the
> hope laid up for you in heaven, of which you
> previously heard in the word of truth, the gospel
> which has come to you, just as in all the world
> also it is constantly bearing fruit and increasing,
> even as it has been doing in you also since the day
> you heard of it and understood the grace of God
> in truth. (Colossians 1:3–6)

The word of God is powerful. When the word is in your heart, it guides your mind and through the Spirit leads you to bear fruit for God. The Word of God, the Bible, works in our hearts and leads us to be obedient. In his letter to the Thessalonians, Paul stated this idea again.

> For this reason we also constantly thank God that
> when you received the word of God which you
> heard from us, you accepted it not as the word of
> men, but for what it really is, the word of God,
> which also performs its work in you who believe.
> (1 Thessalonians 2:13)

The word of God itself bears fruit and works in us who believe, so it is highly important that we spend time in the Scriptures, reading and studying and allowing them to penetrate deeply. These passages show how important bearing fruit is to God. He wants everyone to be saved. We have been blessed with saving grace and a relationship with God, the Father, and His Son, Jesus Christ. We have the Holy Spirit of God living within us. We cannot keep this to ourselves. Everything we have, everything we are, belongs to Him. He has freely blessed us, and we should freely bless others. This really should be our primary aim, after loving God. Jesus said that the greatest commandment is to love the Lord your God with all of your heart, with all of your mind, with all of your soul, and with all of your strength. The second greatest commandment is to love your neighbor as yourself. This is what we are about. Love God and be diligent to know His word and His will and obey it; and love and care for the people who surround you, knowing that what they need most is the love of God in their lives. Take root in God, being well-established in His word and in relationship with Him. Once rooted and grounded in Him, bear fruit for Him. If you don't know what that means for you, ask Him. He has promised that He will answer you so that you may bear fruit. There is a wonderful poem by Rudyard Kipling that is very fitting to close out this book. It is entitled *The Glory of the Garden*; and while written about England and has clear political undertones, I feel it still speaks to the theme of this book, with God as the Gardener and we the workers in His Garden.

"The Glory of the Garden"
By Rudyard Kipling

Our England is a garden that is full of stately views,
Of borders, beds and shrubberies and lawns and
    avenues,
With statues on the terraces and peacocks strut-
    ting by;
But the Glory of the Garden lies in more than
    meets the eye.
For where the old thick laurels grow, along the
    thin red wall,
You will find the tool- and potting-sheds which
    are the heart of all;
The cold-frames and the hot-houses, the dung-
    pits and the tanks:
The rollers, carts and drain-pipes, with the bar-
    rows and the planks.
And there you'll see the gardeners, the men and
    'prentice boys
Told off to do as they are bid and do it without
    noise;

For, except when seeds are planted and we shout
to scare the birds,
The Glory of the Garden it abideth not in words.
And some can pot begonias and some can bud
a rose,
And some are hardly fit to trust with anything
that grows;
But they can roll and trim the lawns and sift the
sand and loam,
For the Glory of the Garden occupieth all who
come.
Our England is a garden, and such gardens are
not made
By singing:—"Oh, how beautiful!" and sitting in
the shade,
While better men than we go out and start their
working lives
At grubbing weeds from gravel-paths with bro-
ken dinner-knives.
There's not a pair of legs so thin, there's not a
head so thick,
There's not a hand so weak and white, nor yet a
heart so sick.
But it can find some needful job that's crying to
be done,
For the Glory of the Garden glorifieth every one.
Then seek your job with thankfulness and work
till further orders,
If it's only netting strawberries or killing slugs on
borders;
And when your back stops aching and your hands
begin to harden,
You will find yourself a partner in the Glory of
the Garden.
Oh, Adam was a gardener, and God who made
him sees

That half a proper gardener's work is done upon
    his knees,
So when your work is finished, you can wash
    your hand and pray
For the Glory of the Garden, that it may not pass
    away!
And the Glory of the Garden it shall never pass
    away![56]

It all started in a garden, a place of beauty and serenity, with the tree of life at its center, where God walked among His creation and intimately communed with Adam and Eve. It was a place of peace and harmony and a perfect relationship between God and man. It was in a garden where Jesus agonized over the suffering He was about to endure; a suffering and ultimate victory over sin that would bring us back into intimate communion with God. His resurrection sealed that deal. And in the eternal garden, where the tree of life still bears its fruit, we will once again live in a perfect relationship with our God forever. So whether you are a strawberry, a rake, or a bumblebee, use what you have been given to bless and encourage those around you. In this way we, as the body of Christ, become a beautiful garden, taking root downward into the soil of the Word and bearing fruit upward to the glory of God.

---

[56] Rudyard Kipling, *The Glory of the Garden*, accessed February 23, 2021, https://public-domain-poetry.com/rudyard-kipling, Puttock International Pty. Ltd., © 2005.

Questions to Consider

Chapter 14: The Harvest

1. Using the garden metaphor, how would you classify yourself: a shovel, a water bucket, a bee...? Explain.

_____

_____

_____

_____

_____

2. How important is it to God that we bear fruit? Explain.

_____

_____

_____

_____

_____

3. How does repentance relate to bearing fruit (Matthew 3:7–10)?

_____

_____

_____

_____

_____

4. How does the word of God bear fruit in and of itself (Colossians 1:3–6; 1 Thessalonians 2:13)?

_____

_____

_____

_____

Using the lines below, write out 2 Corinthians 9:10–11. Reread it many times during the week. Try to commit it to memory.

_____

_____

_____

_____

_____

_____

_____

_____

_____

_____

_____

_____

_____

_____

_____

_____

_____

_____

_____

_____

_____

_____

_____

_____

_____

_____

Father,

Thank You for being our God and Father. Show us how to be effective in bearing fruit for You. Give us a penitent and submissive heart to serve You. In Jesus's name, amen.

BIBLIOGRAPHY

Bloom, Jon. "It's Not a Talent Show." March 14, 2016. *DesiringGod. org*. March 10, 2021.

Bonhoeffer, Dietrich. *The Cost of Discipleship*. United States: Touchstone, 2012.

Bridges, Jerry. *The Practice of Godliness*. Colorado Springs: Navpress, 1983.

Browning, Elizabeth Barrett. *How Do I Love Thee? (Sonnet 43)*. Public Domain.

Byrne, Mary and Eleanor Hull. "Be Thou My Vision." Public Domain.

Edwards, Jonathan. *A Treatise Concerning Religious Affections*. Dublin: J. Ogle, 1812.

—. *Charity and Its Fruits: Or, Christian Love as Manifested in the Heart and Life*. United Kingdom: Rober Carter & Brothers, 1852.

—. "Dissertation of the End for Which God Created the World." *The Complete Works of Jonathan Edwards*.

—. "Sermon 12 on Charity: Willing to Undergo Sufferings for Christ." 1996–2021. *A Puritan's Mind*. www.apuritansmind.com.

Gerson, Charlotte. "Food Matters." n.d. *Foodmatters.tv*. February 18, 2021.

Heath, Brandon. "Hands of the Healer." By Thad Cockrell and Brandon Heath. Prod. Dan Muckala, 2012.

Holy Bible, New International Version. Copyright Ó 1973, 1978, 1984 International Bible Society. Used by permission of Zondervan Bible Publishers.

Google's English Dictionary—Oxford Languages, 2020.

Jekyll, Gertrude. *Gertrude Jekyll on Gardening*. Vintage Books, 1985.

Kenyon, Archibald. "Peace in Jesus." Public Domain.

Kipling, Rudyard. *The Glory of the Garden*. publicdomainpoetry.com.

Knost, L. R. *Two Thousand Kisses a Day: Gentle Parenting through the Ages and Stages*. Little Hearts Books, LLC, 2013.

Lee, Jennifer. *The Book of Quotes*. 2020.

Littauer, Florence. *It Takes So Little to Be Above Average*. Harvest House Publishers, 1996.

Longfellow, Henry Wadsworth. "The Village Blacksmith." n.d. *Poets. org*. Academy of American Poets, February 4, 2021. http:// www.poets.org.

MacArthur, John. "The Fruit of the Spirit, part 3." 2021. *Grace to You*. gty.org.

—. *The Gospel According to Jesus*. Zondervan, 2008.

—. "Winning by Losing: The Paradox of Discipleship, Sermon #2321." October 24, 1982. *Grace to You*. March 10, 2021. gty.org.

Manning, Brennan. *The Wisdom of Tenderness*. Harper One, 2010.

Mayo Clinic. "Narcissistic Personality Disorder." 1998–2021. *Mayo Foundation for Medical Education and Research*, March 10, 2021.

Merriam-Webster. *Merriam-Webster.com/dictionary*. February 23, 2021.

Neal, Patrick. "The Baby Boomers Were Nicknamed the 'Me Generation' Due to their Perceived Narcissism." *The Vintage News*, September 5, 2016.

New American Standard Bible. ® Copyright Ó 1960, 1962, 1963, 1968, 1971, 1973, 1975, 1977, 1995 by the Lockman Foundation. Used by permission. www.lockman.org.

Piper, John. "How Do You Define Joy?" July 25, 2015. *DesiringGod. org*. March 10, 2021.

—. "The Fierce Fruit of Self-Control." May 15, 2001. *Desiring God*. February 6, 2021. http://www.desiringGod.org.

Robert Louis Stevenson Quotes. n.d. 2021 Brainy Media Inc. <http://www. brainyquote.com/quotes/robert_louis_stevenson_101230.>.

Singh, Awdhesh. *31 Ways to Happiness*. Wisdom Tree, 2019.

Spurgeon, Charles Haddon. "Christ and His Co-workers." *Metropolitan Tabernacle Pulpit*. June 10, 1886.

—. "Divine Sovereignty." *New Park Street Pulpit*. May 4, 1856.

—. *Humility and How to Get It*. Tyndale Bible Society, 1970.

—. "The Talking Book." *Metropolitan Tabernacle Pulpit*. October 21, 1871.

—. "Unto the End." *The Sword and the Trowel*. January 1882.

Stein, Joel. "The Me Me Me Generation." *Time Magazine*, May 20, 2013.

The Ultimate Book of Quotations. Lulu.com.

Vine, W. E. *Vine's Expository Dictionary of Biblical Words*. Thomas Nelson Publishers, 1985.

Tozer, A. W. *The Knowledge of the Holy*. Harper Collins, 1978.

—. *The Pursuit of God: The Human Thirst for the Divine*. Bethany House, 2013.

—. *Worship: The Missing Jewel*. Heritage Series, Christian Publications, 1992.

Winger, Mike. *Can I Trust Bible Translations: Evidence for the Bible, part 17*. November 11, 2016. YouTube video, March 10, 2021.

ABOUT THE AUTHOR

L. Maxwell Owen was born and raised in Portland, Oregon, in the beautiful Pacific Northwest. Her parents, Elmer and Edna Maxwell, instilled in her a love for God and His church. She was blessed with a Christian education from first grade on through high school at Columbia Christian Schools. There she began her studies into the word of God. She graduated with honors from Columbia Christian College a few years later with a degree in elementary education.

For the next thirty years or so, Mrs. Owen taught in the public school system. Over the years, she taught many different subjects and ages, but the majority of her time was spent in a sixth-grade classroom at Boring Middle School in Boring, Oregon. She retired from teaching in 2018.

Mrs. Owen currently lives with her husband, Ken, in Boring, Oregon, where they enjoy their country home in the shadow of Mt. Hood. There she spends her time working in their garden: planting, harvesting, canning, and sharing in the bounty it produces. She also enjoys artistic endeavors: drawing, painting, and wood carving. Music is also an important aspect of her life as she loves singing and playing the mandolin.

Mrs. Owen has always had a love for writing. She has journaled most of her life, and writing has become an outlet for her thoughts and feelings. She became a follower of Jesus Christ at a young age and is enthralled by the Word of God. Throughout her life, she has had a love for God and His word.